Dining In—Miami

COOKBOOK

Cover photography: Fred Milkie
Edited by Steve Raichlen
Food: Dave Holt, Steve Debaste, and Robert Z. Tate
Table Setting: Panache, Seattle, WA. 98104
Production and Illustration: Sue Irwin
Typesetting: Julie Lloyd, Angus McGill

Dining In—Miami
COOKBOOK

A Collection of Gourmet Recipes for Complete Meals from the Miami Area's Finest Restaurants

BARBARA SELDIN KLEIN

Edited by
STEVE RAICHLEN

Peanut Butter Publishing
Seattle, Washington

TITLES IN SERIES

Dining In–Baltimore
Dining In–Boston
Dining In–Chicago, Vol. I
Dining In–Chicago, Vol. II
Dining In–Chicago, Vol. III
Dining In–Cleveland
Dining In–Dallas
Dining In–Denver
Dining In–Hampton Roads
Dining In–Hawaii
Dining In–Houston, Vol. I
Dining In–Houston, Vol. II
Dining In–Kansas City
Dining In–Los Angeles
Dining In–Miami
Dining In–Manhattan
Dining In–Milwaukee
Dining In–Minneapolis/St. Paul, Vol. I
Dining In–Minneapolis/St: Paul, Vol. II
Dining In–Monterey Peninsula
Dining In–New Orleans
Dining In–Philadelphia
Dining In–Phoenix
Dining In–Pittsburgh
Dining In–Portland
Dining In–St. Louis
Dining In–Salt Lake City
Dining In–San Francisco, Vol. I
Dining In–San Francisco, Vol. II
Dining In–Seattle, Vol. I
Dining In–Seattle, Vol. II
Dining In–Seattle, Vol. III
Dining In–Sun Valley
Dining In–Toronto
Dining In–Vancouver, B.C.
Dining In–Washington, D.C.

DEDICATION

This book is dedicated to the memory of my father,
Phil Seldin
who, if he knew, would be so proud.

ACKNOWLEDGEMENTS

I am a great believer that, "No man walks alone." For this book I wish to thank, first and foremost my children. Jake and Betsy for their love and understanding and eating those endless sandwiches, while I was out Dining In-Miami. Janis Bacus (my good luck charm) for being there when it all began. Elliott Wolf, my publisher, who believed in me and kept my spirits up. To Carol Kotkin, (my mentor) who inspired me with my very first cooking class. To Terry Zarikian for Dining In-Miami with me and commiserating about every meal.

To Michael Klein, for his never ending cash flow for without which this book might have never been written. To Eileen Nexer for her spiritual guidance. And to my mother Miriam Seldin, just for being mom.

A special thanks to the restaurants who fed me every dish in this book and to the chefs who supplied the recipes.

And last and certainly not least to Steven Raichlen (my Cambridge Prince) for teaching me my P's and Q's—among other things.

CONTENTS

Preface . . . . *xi*
Cafe Chauveron 1
Casa Juancho 9
Christine Lee's Gaslight 17
The Dining Galleries 25
Dominique's 31
El Sevilla 39
The Forge 47
The Grand Cafe 59
Il Tulipano 67
Joe's Stone Crab 77
La Scala 83
Le Festival 91
The Miami Palm 97
New York Steak House 103
The Pavillon Grill 111
Raimondo's 119
Regine's 127
The Spoonbill 137
Tiberio 143
Veronique's 151
Vinton's 159
About the Author *169*
Recipe Index *171*

PREFACE

When I was asked to write Dining In–Miami I was thrilled at the opportunity to tell you about Miami's most talked about restaurants. I sense an excitement taking place in Miami and I am glad to be a part of it.

All of the restaurants in this book are highly touted for one reason or another. Some are old-time institutions, others are the trendsetters of today. They will all provide you with an evening of dining pleasure; what they won't provide you with is an interesting dining partner; for that you are on your own.

Barbara Seldin

Cafe Chauveron

Dinner For Six

Les Huitres Chauveron

Les Cuisses de Grenouille Provençale

Les Côtes de Veau Bercy

Pommes Soufflée

Wines:

With the Frog Legs — Puligny Montrachet, 1982

With the Veal Chops — Chateau Lascombes, 1971

With the Soufflé — "Cuvée Special" Champagne

Andre Chauveron, Owner

Miami's legendary Cafe Chauveron has been half a century in the making. The year was 1935; the place was 49th street and Third Avenue in New York City; the man was French-born Roger Chauveron, who founded first the Café Chambord and then the Cafe Chauveron. In 1972, Roger moved his family—and his restaurant—to Miami Beach, and the Bay Harbor Cafe Chauveron was born.

Today, the restaurant is in its second generation, run by Roger's only son, Andre. But the bill of fare remains faithful to the classic French cuisine of the founder. House specialties reflect the Perigordine heritage of the Chauveron family. (Perigord is a region in southwest France, famed for its *foie gras*, goose, and truffles.) Highpoints of the extensive menu include seafood crêpes, flambé/duckling with Grand Marnier sauce, *pommes soufflés* (soufflé potatoes) and feather-light dessert soufflés.

The Cafe sits on Bay Harbor Island, overlooking Saks Fifth Avenue and Indian Creek (which makes the restaurant accessible by yacht). The Chauveron seats 200 in its two dining rooms and can serve that many soufflés a night. Wines dating back to 1927 are housed in a handsome, climate-controlled glass chamber. The service is gracious and attentive: over 90% of the staff is French.

Cafe owner Andre Chauveron is the opposite of the typical Frenchman. When I asked him what makes the Cafe better than other Miami restuarants, he answered, "We are not better; we are all good in Miami; only our styles are different." And this busy Miami restauranteur still finds time to volunteer as a waiter at his childrens' camp!

9561 East Bay Harbor Drive
Bay Harbor Island

LES HUITRES CHAUVERON
(Oysters Chauveron)

1 stick butter, softened
4 shallots, finely chopped
4 cloves garlic, finely chopped
1 bunch fresh parsley, stems removed, finely chopped

1 tablespoon Pernod
Salt and pepper to taste
3 dozen oysters, shucked and cleaned

1. Cream the butter, and whisk in the remaining ingredients except the oysters. Top each oyster with a spoonful of the butter mixture. Place oysters on a baking sheet and bake in a 400° oven for 5 minutes, or until the butter is bubbly and the oysters are cooked.

Pernod is an anise-flavored aperitif popular in France. It is available in any major liquor store, or you can substitute Anisette.

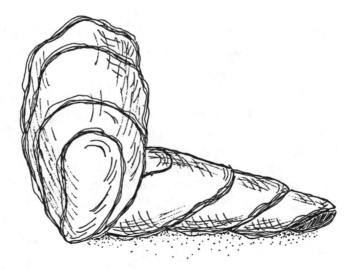

LES CUISSES DE GRENOUILLES PROVENÇALE
(Frog Legs Provençale)

2 dozen frog legs
1 cup milk
Flour for dusting
Salt and fresh black pepper
12 tablespoons butter
2 tablespoons oil

6 cloves garlic, finely chopped
½ cup dry white wine
½ pound tomatoes, peeled, seeded, and chopped*
2 tablespoons chopped parsley

1. Dip the legs in milk and dust with flour, salt, and pepper. Heat 4 tablespoons butter and the oil in a large frying pan, and sauté the frog legs until golden brown. Remove from pan and pour off all but 3 tablespoons fat.

2. Add the garlic and shallots and sauté for one minute. Add the white wine and reduce by half. Add the remaining 8 tablespoons of butter, the tomatoes, and parsley, and simmer for 2 minutes. Add salt and pepper to taste. Pour the sauce over the frog legs and serve at once.

In most cities, French restuarants serve frozen frog legs. Not in Miami. Our proximity to the Everglades makes it easy to get fresh frog legs. That is the secret to this dish.

TO PEEL, SEED, AND CHOP TOMATOES

*To peel and seed tomatoes, cut out the stem end, cut a small X on the bottom, and plunge the tomatoes in rapidly boiling water for 30 seconds. Rinse under cold water: the skin will slip off easily. Cut the tomatoes in half widthwise and wring them out by squeezing the halves in the palms of your hands. Cut to the desired consistency.

LES COTES DE VEAU BERCY
(Veal Chop with Sauce Bercy)

6 (12-ounce) veal chops
Flour for dusting
Salt and pepper
4 tablespoons oil
8 tablespoons butter

¾ cup very finely chopped shallots
1 cup dry white wine
2 cups BROWN SAUCE

1. Dust the veal chops with flour, salt, and pepper. Heat the oil and 4 tablespoons of butter in a large frying pan until foaming. Add the chops and sauté for 1 minute per side or until golden brown. Remove from pan and keep warm.

2. Pour off all but 3 tablespoons fat. Add the shallots and sauté for 1 minute. Add the wine and boil until only ¼ cup liquid remains. Add the *BROWN SAUCE* and bring to a boil. Add 4 tablespoons butter and shake the pan back and forth until it is mixed in. Correct the seasoning and pour the sauce over the veal chops. Serve at once.

Shallots have a taste that is a cross between onions and garlic. There is no substitute. Do not let them burn when sautéing, or they will become bitter.

Bercy—a neighborhood in Paris—was formerly the center of the wine trade. Thus a dish with the name Bercy contains white wine and shallots.

BROWN SAUCE

4 veal knuckles
2 carrots, sliced
2 large onions, unpeeled, quartered
2 celery stalks, sliced
½ teaspoon dried thyme
1 bay leaf

3 parsley sprigs
1 cup dry white wine
4 quarts cold water
4 tablespoons tomato paste
Salt
Whole black peppercorns
3 tablespoons cornstarch

1. Put the bones and vegetables in a roasting pan and roast them in a 400° oven for 1 hour until thoroughly browned. Transfer the bones and vegetables to a stockpot, and add all remaining ingredients except the cornstarch. Slowly bring the stock to a boil, reduce the heat, and simmer for 4 hours. Skim any residue that rose to the top, as necessary.*

2. Strain the stock and bring it to a boil. Combine three tablespoons cornstarch with three tablespoons of cold water, and stir into the boiling stock. Simmer for a few minutes, and remove from heat.

It is very important to skim the stock as it cooks. If you don't, the end product will be cloudy.

Brown sauce is nothing more than veal stock thickened with a little cornstarch. This recipe will make 2 quarts. The excess can be frozen in 1 cup containers for future use.

POMMES SOUFFLES
(Soufflé Potatoes)

6 Idaho potatoes   2 quarts frying oil

1. Peel the potatoes and carefully cut off the sides, top, and bottom to form elongated cubes. Cut each cube into ⅛ inch slices.

2. Heat the oil in two pans, one to 300°, and one to 400°. Cook the potatoes in several batches in the moderately hot oil, shaking the pan gently to keep the slices moving. When they begin to puff, transfer them to the hot oil. They will puff fully. Remove at once with a slotted spoon, and drain on paper towels.

3. Just before serving, heat the soufflé potatoes in hot oil.

You must use baking potatoes. They must be cut into slices exactly ⅛ inch thick.

Soufflé potatoes were one of those great dishes that began as an accident. King Louis-Philippe was due to ride on the newly invented railroad. At the

end of the line in St. Germain, the royal chef was to greet him with a banquet. At the appointed hour, the chef plunged his potatoes in hot fat to make what the French call "game chips." But the king's train was late, so the chef was unable to serve them. When the king finally appeared, the chef reheated the potatoes in oil, and <u>voila!</u>: they puffed like pillows. Thus, a new dish was born.

SOUFFLE AU CHOCOLAT
(Chocolate Soufflé)

¼ pound sweet chocolate
1 cup milk
2½ tablespoons sugar
3 tablespoons flour

6 eggs, separated
½ teaspoon vanilla extract
1 teaspoon butter

1. Prepare a 1 quart soufflé dish by thoroughly buttering the inside and sprinkling with sugar. Preheat the oven to 450°.

2. Combine the chocolate and milk in a 1 quart saucepan, stirring frequently, until the chocolate melts. Remove the pan from the heat. Combine the sugar and flour in a bowl, add the egg yolks and whisk until the mixture is very creamy. Slowly stir in the melted chocolate and milk. Return this mixture to the saucepan and cook it over medium heat, stirring constantly, until the sauce is smooth and thick. Stir in the vanilla and butter.

3. Beat the egg whites to stiff peaks, and fold them gently into the chocolate mixture. Spoon this mixture into the prepared soufflé dish. Bake the soufflé in the hot oven for 20 to 30 minutes, or until puffed and browned.

 # Casa Juancho

Dinner For Six

Sangria

Sopa De Ajo Castellana

Tortilla a la Española

Paella

Leche Frita

Beverage:

Sangria

Felipe Valls, Owner

9

Make no mistake: the Casa Juancho is not a Cuban restaurant, although it is located in the heart of "Little Havana." It is 100 percent Spanish, from the menu to the staff to the decor. It is, in fact, the only restaurant I know that serves *Tapas*, Spanish hor d'oeuvres.

Stepping into the Casa Juancho is like entering a medieval house in Castille. Architect Jose Maria de la Guerra decorated the restaurant with terracotta tile floors, rough-hewn rafters, hanging cauldrons, and massive clay pots. Hanging from the ceiling beams are strings of peppers, wreathes of garlic, and *Serrano* (country) hams.

Good smells emanate from the open kitchen next to the bar, where an army of chefs prepare tortillas (Spanish omelettes), *Langostinos al ajillo* (shrimp with garlic), and other Spanish delicacies. Menu listings come from all over Spain: *Paella* from Valencia on the Mediterranean, garlic soup from the Castille, and *Leche Frite*—fried pastry cream—from the Basque country.

From the minute it opened, in December, 1984, the Casa Juancho has been a smashing success. Consequently, expect a 1-2 hour wait for a table. The mood is festive—the strolling accordianist gets customers singing Spanish, Mexican, and even Hebrew songs. Casa Juancho's success is attributed to the total Spanish dining experience. They must be doing something right; the restaurant serves 700-900 meals a day.

2436 S.W. 8th Street

SANGRIA

2 bottles, dry red
  wine
3 ounces brandy
3 ounces triple sec
2 oranges, cut into wedges

2 limes, cut into wedges
1 apple, cored and cut into
  wedges
3 cups ice
1 quart Seven-Up or other
  lemon-lime soda

1. Combine all ingredients except the Seven-Up in a large bowl and let seep for 1 hour. To serve, place ice in a pitcher and then fill it with wine mixture, adding Seven-Up to taste.

Sangria, so the story goes, was invented in old Castille. It should be made with a strong red wine, preferably one of Spanish origins. Sangria is by far the most popular drink in Spain, served whenever there is a festive occasion.

SOPA DE AJO CASTILLIANA
(Garlic Soup)

3 ounces fresh garlic
  (approximately 3 heads)
6 ounces Spanish country
  ham
4 tablespoons olive oil
6 thin slices bread
2 tablespoons Spanish
  paprika

3 quarts chicken stock or
  beef stock (see recipes
  on page 166)
Salt
6 eggs, lightly beaten

1. Peel the garlic cloves. (To facilitate peeling the individual cloves, pound them lightly with the side of a cleaver.) Cut the garlic into thin slices. Cut the ham into thin slivers.

2. Heat the olive oil in a large saucepan. Add the garlic and cook over medium heat for 3 minutes or until golden brown. Add the ham slices and cook for 1 minute. Add the bread slices and lightly brown on both sides. Stir in the paprika and cook for 1 minute.

3. Add the stock and simmer the soup for 5 minutes. Correct the seasoning with salt and pepper. Just before serving whisk in the beaten eggs, little by little. (The result should resemble Chinese eggdrop soup.) Garlic soup is traditionally served in earthenware bowls.

Garlic soup is one of the most famous Castillian dishes. In Spain it is sometimes served for breakfast—it is reported to be an excellent remedy for hangovers. The garlic looses its pungency when cooked.

TORTILLA A LA ESPAÑOLA
(Spanish Style Omelette)

4 *pounds onions*	*Salt and fresh black pepper*
6 *pounds potatoes*	12 *eggs*
2 *cups olive oil*	

1. Cut the onions into thin slices. Peel and thinly slice the potatoes.

2. Heat all but 4 tablespoons oil in one very large or two large frying pans. Cook the onions over medium heat for 5 minutes. Add the potato slices and salt and pepper to taste, and cook another 5-8 minutes, or until the potatoes are soft. Transfer the onions and potatoes to a colander and drain off the oil. Thoroughly beat the eggs in a large bowl and stir in the vegetables.

3. Heat the remaining 4 tablespoons oil in a large frying pan over high heat. The oil should be very hot. Add the omelette mixture to the pan and cook over medium heat for 3-4 minutes, or until golden brown. If you are feeling adept, flip the tortilla with a flick of the wrist. Alternately, place a large plate over the frying pan, invert the tortilla onto the plate, and slide it, uncooked side down, back into the frying pan. Cook the other side for 4 minutes, or until golden brown. Cut into wedges and serve at once.

This recipe will actually serve 6 people as an entree. For an appetizer, cut the recipe in half.

A Spanish tortilla is not a corn flour flatcake, but an onion and potato-studded omelette. This dish is best made in a well-seasoned cast iron frying pan.

PAELLA

½ cup olive oil
6 ounces green pepper, diced
4 cloves garlic, minced
4 ounces onion, diced
8 ounces chicken, cut into 2-inch pieces
6 clams
6 mussels
8 ounces lobster
8 ounces monkfish, cut into 1-inch pieces
8 ounces squid, cleaned and cut into rings
2 cups rice
½ teaspoon saffron
8 ounces sweet red pepper, diced
1 cup fresh peas
¾ cup tomato sauce
3 cups chicken stock
Fresh lemon, for garnish

1. Heat the oil in the paella pan. Sauté the pepper, garlic and onion over medium heat for 2 minutes, but do not let brown. Add the chicken pieces, shellfish, monkfish, squid, and rice, and sauté for 1 minute, or until the rice is coated with oil and shiny.

2. Meanwhile, grind the saffron in a mortar and pestle, moistening it with a little stock. (Note: this step is optional. If you are in a hurry, add the saffron directly to the frying pan.) Add the saffron to the pan, with the remaining ingredients. Bring the liquid to a boil, and gently simmer for 5 minutes.

3. Place the paella in a preheated 400° oven and cook for 20-30 minutes, or until the rice is soft and the liquid is absorbed. Serve at once, with fresh lemon for squeezing.

Saffron is the world's most expensive spice. A little goes a long way.

Paella is traditionally cooked in a special pan called a paellera. A paellera is a large, flat, open pan with outwardly sloping sides and handles. It resembles a giant pie plate. If you don't have a paellera, you can use a large, heavy-gauge frying pan. The important thing is that the depth of rice not be more than 2½ inches, otherwise it will be soggy.

LECHE FRITA

1 quart milk
2 cinnamon sticks
   Zest from one orange
   Zest from one lemon
6 tablespoons cornstarch
2 cups sugar
4 eggs

1 tablespoon butter (for
   frying fish)
1 cup flour (for dipping)
2 eggs, beaten
1-2 cups oil, for frying
2 cinnamon sticks
   powdered

1. Place the milk, cinnamon sticks, and citrus peel in a heavy saucepan and gently simmer over low heat for 5 minutes. Remove the cinnamon sticks and place the cornstarch and 1½ cups sugar in a large bowl and beat in the 4 eggs.

2. Strain the milk into the egg mixture, whisking vigorously. Return the mixture to the pan and cook it over medium heat for 5 minutes, whisking vigorously to prevent it from sticking. (Note: you must whisk vigorously—this mixture has a tendency to stick and burn.)

3. Pour the custard mixture into a lightly buttered baking dish. It should be no more than ½-inch thick. Chill in the refrigerator for at least 4 hours, preferably overnight.

4. Just before serving, cut the chilled custard into 3-inch squares. Dip each square first in flour, then in beaten egg. Heat the oil to 375° in a frying pan. Fry the custard squares in the oil until golden brown on both sides. Combine the ½ cup sugar and cinnamon and sprinkle it over *leche frita* for serving.

This dish comes from the Basque region of Spain. Not surprisingly, it is French in origin, consisting of crème patissière (pastry cream) that is chilled, cut into squares, and fried. The zest is the oil-rich outer peel of a citrus fruit—it is best removed with a vegetable peeler or special zesting tool.

Christine Lee's GASLIGHT

Dinner For Six

Coconut Shrimp

Eggplant Imperial

Lemon Chicken

Szechuan–Style Sliced Fish

Beverage:

Before Dinner—Singapore Sling

With Dinner—Tea

Christine Lee, Owner

There are many Chinese restaurants in Miami, but in the words of Billy Joel, there is only one Christine Lee. Christine Lee has received national attention ever since she turned her living room in New Jersey into a restaurant in 1961. She was touted by movie stars, acclaimed by food critics, and loved by everyone. Christine moved her Gaslight Restaurant, as it was called in New Jersey, to Miami Beach in 1970, and she has been packing them in ever since.

Enter Christine Lee's through the double doors in the lobby of the Thunderbird Motel. Seat either in the main dining room, with its etched glass and mirrored ceiling, or the lounge, where the bar is standing room only.

Start off your meal with the coconut shrimp. Other house specialties are eggplant imperial and veal Oriental. But don't for one minute think that because this is a Chinese restaurant you can't get a world famous prime sirloin steak. Remember, this *is* Christine Lee's.

Life wasn't always like this for the "Shanghai Eyeful," the nickname columnist Earl Wilson gave her in New York, when she was hostess at the trendy Ruby Foo's. Christine Lee was born a poor girl in Taiwan, raised in Shanghai, and married in Japan. After a brief and unhappy sojourn in San Francisco, she moved to New York, where her life finally turned around.

Christine Lee's Gaslight restaurant opened in the Golden Strand Motel in 1970. Ten years ago, she moved to the present location at the Thunderbird Motel. Hers is truly an American success story. After all, I don't know any other Chinese restaurant that packs the bar three deep. . . I guess it's only Christine Lee.

18401 Collins Avenue

COCONUT SHRIMP

1 pound shrimp, shelled
 and deveined
2 4-ounce packages
 shredded coconut
1 egg
¾ cup milk

¼ cup firmly packed light
 brown sugar
1¼ cups all-purpose flour
2-3 cups vegetable oil,
 for frying

1. Cut each shrimp in half lengthwise. Place the shredded coconut in a shallow bowl.

2. Prepare the batter. In a small bowl, combine the egg, milk and sugar, beating until well blended. Gradually work in the flour, beating with a rotary mixer until smooth.

3. Pour 1 inch of oil into the pan and heat it to 375°. Dip each shrimp half in the egg mixture, then in the coconut (it should be thoroughly coated), then fry in hot oil for 5 minutes, or until golden brown. The shrimp can be reheated in a 350° oven for 5 minutes: they should be served hot.

The best shrimp to use for this recipe are mediums, which come 20 to a pound. The shrimp can be fried in a wok, a deep saucepan, or an electric frying pan.

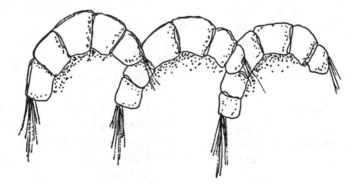

EGGPLANT IMPERIAL

4 Chinese eggplants, or
  2 regular eggplants
1 large green bell pepper
1 large red pepper
6 ounces pork tenderloin
  (or other lean cut)
2 scallions
1 tablespoon dark soy sauce
2 tablespoons light soy
  sauce

½ cup chicken broth
1 tablespoon vinegar
1½ teaspoons sugar
1 teaspoon finely chopped
  garlic
2 teaspoons cornstarch
1 teaspoon sherry
1½ cups peanut oil, for
  frying

1. Peel the eggplant and cut it diagonally into pieces the size and shape of French fries. Core and seed the peppers and cut them into very fine slivers. Cut the pork into matchstick-shaped sticks. Chop the scallion and reserve. Combine the remaining ingredients, except the peanut oil, to make a sauce, reserving ½ teaspoon garlic.

2. Heat all but ¼ cup oil in a wok, and fry the eggplant slices over high heat for 3-4 minutes, or until completely cooked. Transfer the eggplant to a colander, then rinse it off under hot water to wash away the oil. Discard the oil. Add the remaining ¼ cup oil to the wok and heat it over high heat. Stir-fry the pork with the ½ teaspoon garlic for 1 minute. Add the slivered peppers and continue to stir-fry for 1 minute. Thoroughly mix the sauce and add it to the wok with the eggplant. Cook the mixture, stirring until the sauce thickens. Add the scallions, mix well, and serve.

Sometimes I add ½ teaspoon sesame oil, which imparts a pleasant nutty taste. Make sure the cornstarch is thoroughly dissolved.

This dish tastes best made with Chinese eggplants, which are long and slender and have a bright purple skin. If these are unavailable, use regular eggplants, but be sure to peel them. The ingredients can be cut and measured well ahead of time, but they should be cooked at the last minute.

LEMON CHICKEN

6 boneless, skinless chicken breasts	½ teaspoon baking powder
Salt	1 egg
Pepper	1⅓ cups water
2-3 cups oil, for frying	½ cup sweet orange marmalade
1 cup self-rising flour	½ cup lemonade concentrate
½ cup chestnut flour (or cornstarch)	2-3 cups oil, for frying

1. Trim the chicken breasts of any fat and sinew. Season each piece with salt and pepper.

2. Prepare the batter. Combine the flours and baking powder in a bowl. Beat the egg with the water, and quickly beat these liquid ingredients into the dry ones.

3. In a double boiler, combine the marmalade and lemonade concentrate to make a sauce. Mix until smooth. Heat.

4. Heat the oil to 375° in a shallow frying pan. Dip the chicken breasts in the batter and place them in the oil. Reduce the heat to 325° and fry the breasts, turning frequently, for 2-3 minutes, or until golden brown. Pour the heated sauce over the chicken breasts and serve at once.

This traditional Chinese chicken dish owes its lightness to the batter, which contains chestnut flour (made from dried chestnuts. It is available in Chinese grocery stores; in its absence, substitute cornstarch.

SZECHUAN-STYLE SLICED FISH

1 pound fresh red snapper
   or grouper
1 teaspoon cornstarch
1 egg white
1 teaspoon peanut oil
1 ounce tree ears
1 large red bell pepper
2 ounces snow peas
1 inch peeled ginger root

1 scallion
1 teaspoon minced garlic
2 tablespoons soy sauce
½ cup chicken broth
½ tablespoon sugar
½ tablespoon vinegar
1 tablespoon cornstarch
1 tablespoon sherry
2 cups peanut oil, for frying

1. Slice the fish into pieces ⅓ inch thick and 2 inches square. Combine the fish with the cornstarch, egg white, and 1 teaspoon peanut oil, and let stand for 20 minutes. Cover the tree ears with warm water and let stand for 20 minutes.

2. Core and seed the red pepper and cut it into 1 inch squares. Snap the snow peas. Rinse the water chestnuts. Cut the ginger into thin slivers, the scallion, into thin slices, and finely chop the garlic. Combine the ingredients for the sauce.

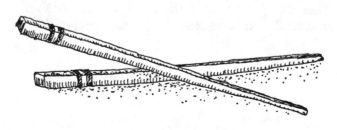

3. Heat the oil in a wok or frying pan—it should be very hot before adding the fish. Add the fish, piece by piece, and cook for 1 minute. Transfer the fish with a slotted spoon to a strainer over a bowl to catch the oil.

4. Discard all but ¼ cup oil from the wok and heat it again. Add the ginger, scallion, and garlic, and stir-fry over high heat for 10 seconds. Add the pepper, water chestnuts, and pea pods, and stir-fry for 1 minute. Add the tree ear and fish. Thoroughly mix the sauce and add it to the wok. Cook the fish, stirring gently, for 1 minute, or until the sauce thickens.

This recipe calls for a slippery black fungus called tree ears in North America, cloud ears in China, and jelly mushrooms in Thailand. Tree ears have very little flavor and are chiefly prized for their slippery, crisp consistency. Available dried at Oriental markets, tree ears will keep indefinitely. They need only be soaked in warm water for 20 minutes before using.

THE DINING GALLERIES

Dinner For Four

Scampi "Dining Galleries"

Native Pompano

Glazed Carrots "Rosa Di Maggio"

Chocolate Dipped Strawberries

Wines:

With the shrimp—Fumé Blanc, Robert Mondavi, V.

With the Fish—Pouilly-Fuissé, Jaboulet-Vercherre, V.

Stephen Muss, Owner

Geoffrey Schober, Executive Chef

An hour's drive from Paris is the village of Fontainebleau, former vacation home of the kings of France. On Collins Avenue in Miami Beach stands the world-famous Fontainebleau Hilton Hotel. It, too, has housed royalty—Frank Sinatra even has a suite named after him.

The Fontainebleau Hilton Dining Galleries lives up to its name, museum quality collection of art. To your left is a bust carved entirely from Carara marble. The *pièce de résistance* is a magnificent Steinway concert grand piano made in Hamburg in 1882.

Masterpieces of an edible sort are prepared at the open appetizer bar, manned by chefs in towering, white toques. Surrounding the bar are huge baskets overflowing with vegetables and fruits. The tables are set with forest green liners, flowered cloths, pink napkins, and flickering candles. Chandeliers sparkle overhead; the walls are lined with mirrors.

Sit back and enjoy the music of Val Ollman on violin and George Blumenthal on piano, while you peruse the green velvet menu. The waiter will offer you a choice of Ramlöse, Evian, or Perrier—there is no tap water at the Galleries. For nibbling, there is *lavoch* and home-baked rolls, not to mention *crudités* served in a glass swan.

For an appetizer, I suggest the *escargots champagne*, snails poached with champagne and leeks and served on a homemade croissant. Parties of four or more should order the "gallerie collection," a lavish spread of hot and cold hor d'oeuvres. Beef-eaters will find the prime rib much to their liking. If fresh Florida pompano should strike your fancy, you won't be alone: it's the best selling dish at the restaurant.

According to food and beverge manager Joseph Rabhan, 70 percent of the clients are locals. And that makes Miami, to paraphrase Frank Sinatra, "my kind of town."

4441 Collins Avenue

SCAMPI "DINING GALLERIES"

12 large shrimp
4 tablespoons butter
1 teaspoon finely chopped
   shallot
1½ teaspoons finely chopped
   garlic
1 teaspoon finely chopped
   tarragon
2 whole tomatoes, peeled,
   seeded, and chopped (see
   instructions on page 4)

½ cup cognac
2 cups LOBSTER BISQUE
   (optional—see
   page 154)
¼ cup heavy cream
   Salt and fresh black
   pepper

1. Peel and devein the shrimp. Melt half the butter in a sauté pan and sauté the shrimp over medium heat for 2 minutes. Transfer the shrimp to a platter and keep warm.

2. Add the remaining butter to the pan, along with the shallots, garlic, tarragon and tomatoes. Sauté for 1 minute. Add the brandy and simmer until reduced by half. Add the lobster bisque, if using, and simmer until reduced by half.

3. Return the shrimp to the sauce and simmer until thoroughly heated. Add the cream and heat, but do not let the sauce boil. Add salt and pepper to taste.

At the Dining Galleries this dish would be made using lobster bisque in the sauce. To simplify the recipe, we have omitted the bisque. Purists will find the recipe for lobster bisque on page 154, should they wish to try the original recipe.

NATIVE POMPANO

2 fresh pompanos
(2½ pounds each)

1 pint milk

1 stick (8 tablespoons)
unsalted butter

1 tablespoon finely
chopped shallots

1 clove garlic, minced

2 ounces fresh mushrooms,
washed and cut in
quarters

4 ounces shelled Alaskan
king crab

1 cup heavy cream

1 teaspoon fresh chopped
chives

Salt and fresh black
pepper

A pinch each chopped basil
and tarragon

Juice of ½ lemon, or
to taste

¾ cup flour, in a shallow
bowl

2 eggs, beaten, in a shallow
bowl

Fresh lemon wedges,
for serving

1. Fillet and skin the pompano, or have your fishmonger do it. Soak the fillets in milk.

2. Meanwhile, melt 4 tablespoons butter in a small frying pan. Add the shallots, garlic, and mushrooms, and sauté over medium heat for 30 seconds. Stir in the crab meat and cook for 15 seconds. Add the cream and chives and simmer for 1 minute, or until thickened. Season the mixture with salt, pepper, basil, tarragon, and lemon juice, then remove from the heat and cool.

3. Remove one pompano fillet from the milk and spread it with the crab mixture. Drain the other fish fillet and press it on top. Dip the fish, on both sides, in flour, shaking off excess. Dip the fish, on both sides, in the beaten egg.

4. Heat the remaining butter in a large sauté pan over high heat. Brown the fish on both sides in the hot butter. Transfer the fish, pan and all, to a preheated 350° oven and bake for 10-15 minutes. Serve with lemon wedges.

Pompano is a firmly-fleshed fish native to Florida waters. If you can't buy this delicacy fresh, substitute red snapper or sole.

GLAZED CARROTS "ROSA DI MAGGIO"

1 pound carrots
1 quart Evian or other
   bottled water
4 tablespoons unsalted
   butter

1 tablespoon finely chopped
   shallots
4 tablespoons sugar
Salt to taste

1. Peel the carrots and cut them on the diagonal into ⅛ inch thick slices. Place the carrots with half the water in a large saucepan. Simmer over a medium heat until the carrots are tender.

2. Meanwhile, melt the butter in another saucepan and cook the shallots over medium heat for 1 minute, or until soft. Do not let brown. Add the sugar and the remaining water. Boil this mixture until the volume is reduced by ¾.

3. Drain the carrots and toss them with the syrup. Add salt to taste and serve at once.

The secret to glazed carrots is the water—Evian in this recipe—but any bottled water will do. The dish is even better when made with new carrots.

CHOCOLATE DIPPED STRAWBERRIES

12 large Driscol strawberries
¼ cup Grand Marnier

½ pound covering chocolate

1. Gently wash the strawberries. Using a cooking syringe (available at gourmet shops), inject each with a little Grand Marnier and refrigerate for 1 hour.

2. Melt the chocolate over a pan of barely simmering water. Dip each strawberry in the melted chocolate, holding it by the stem. (Leave the top ¼ of the berry undipped.) Set the berries to cool on waxed paper. When the chocolate has hardened, peel the waxed paper off and serve.

The best strawberries to use are the large Driscol variety from California. The best chocolate is a Swiss or Brazilian covered chocolate—buy it at a baker's supply shop. Gourmet shops sell special syringes for injecting the berries with booze.

Dominique's
famous french restaurants

Dinner For Four

Green Bean Salad with Truffle Vinaigrette

Shrimp with Ginger Sauce

Medallions of Veal with Wild Musnroom Sauce

Amaretto Soufflé

Wines:

With Dinner and Desert — Bollinger Brut Champagne

Stephen Muss and Dominique D'Ermo, Owners

Henry Sillman, Food and Beverage Manager

Thomas Schraa, Manager

Pacal Oudin, Director

The Alexander is one hotel where you don't have to ask the concierge where to eat. Stay put. The path to gastronomic paradise leads up a sweeping staircase, through a glass enclosed walkway surrounded by tropical plants, to the wrought iron gates of Dominique's.

Alexander was the father of Stephen Muss. Stephen Muss is the owner of Quayside, Fountainbleau-Hilton, and Seacoast Towers. When Mr. Muss opened the Alexander Hotel, he filled it with tapestries, sculptures, Old Master oil paintings, and antiques from the Cornelius Vanderbilt mansion. Then he set out to get Dominique.

Dominique is the fellow in Washington, D.C., who serves rattlesnake, ostrich, camel salad, kangaroo, alligator, buffalo, llama, wild boar, black bear, and roasted hippopotamus. In the unlikely case that none of this appeals to you, take heart. The French born chef also serves quail, pheasant, mallard duck, and baby lambs, which he raises on his farm in Maryland. Still too exotic? There's always New York strip steak, T-bones, and fillet mignon with bearnaise sauce. As for the fish, much of it is flown in on the Concord from Paris.

The tables are set with pink cloths and gold and green rimmed service plates. Chandeliers sparkle overhead. If you like the food, you'll be pleased to know that Dominique cans his own soup and has written three cookbooks: *The Chef's Dessert Cookbook*, *Dominique's Famous Fish, Game and Meat Recipes*, and *The Modern Pastry Chef's Guide to Professional Baking*.

Alexander Hotel
5225 Collins Avenue

GREEN BEAN SALAD WITH TRUFFLE VINAIGRETTE

1½ *pounds slender green*
    beans
    Salt
4 *large mushrooms*
2 *heads Belgian endive*

1 *head radicchio*
  TRUFFLE
  VINAIGRETTE
  (see below)

1. Snap the stem ends off the green beans and pull out any strings. Cook the green beans in at least 3 quarts of rapidly boiling, heavily salted water for 3-4 minutes, or until tender, but still a little crisp. Transfer the beans to a strainer, run under cold water until cool, and drain the beans until dry.

2. Cut the mushrooms into thin slices. Break the Belgian endive into individual leaves. Wash and dry the radicchio. Prepare the dressing.

3. To serve, pile the grean beans in the center of each of four large salad plates. Arrange the sliced mushrooms over the beans. Fan the endive leaves to one side of the beans, and arrange the radicchio to the other. Spoon the *TRUFFLE VINAIGRETTE* on top and serve at once.

In France we would make this salad with haricots verts, *a very thin species of green bean. At Dominique's in Miami we use a slender string bean imported from Guatamala. Naturally, you can use regular green beans, but try to select the smallest ones.*

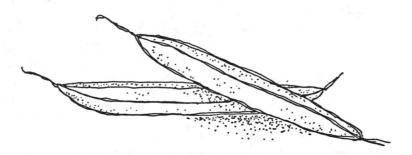

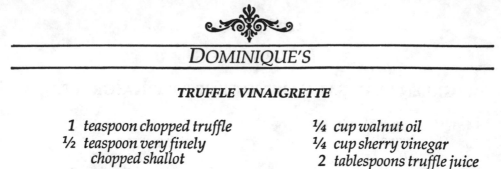

TRUFFLE VINAIGRETTE

1 teaspoon chopped truffle
½ teaspoon very finely
   chopped shallot
2 egg yolks
¾ cup vegetable oil

¼ cup walnut oil
¼ cup sherry vinegar
2 tablespoons truffle juice
   Salt and fresh black pepper

1. Combine the first three ingredients in a large, non-aluminum bowl, and mix well with a whisk.

2. Gradually whisk in the vegetable oil: the sauce should thicken. Gradually whisk in the walnut oil, followed by the remaining ingredients. Correct the seasoning, added salt and fresh black pepper to taste.

A truffle is a golf ball-sized fungus that grows underground in southwest France. Despite their unattractive appearance, fresh truffles cost a king's ransom: up to $400 a pound. Canned truffles, particularly, truffle pieces are less expensive. Be sure to save the flavor-rich juice.

SHRIMP WITH GINGER SAUCE

24 large shrimp
½ pound fresh spinach
4 tablespoons butter
   Salt and pepper

FOR THE SAUCE:

1 stick butter (½ cup)
¼ cup fresh ginger, chopped
2 tablespoons garlic,
   chopped
½ cup honey
1 cup red wine vinegar
2 tablespoons soy sauce
2 tablespoons teriyaki sauce
1 cup DEMI GLACE (see
   recipe on page 55)

1. Peel and devein the shrimp. Stem and wash the spinach and cook it in rapidly boiling, salted water for 30 seconds. Drain the spinach and arrange on plates.

2. Meanwhile prepare the sauce. Melt the butter in a large frying pan and sauté the ginger and garlic for 4 to 5 minutes or until soft but not brown. Add the honey and simmer for 5 minutes or until it reaches the carmel stage.

3. Add the red wine vinegar, soy sauce, teriyaki sauce and boil until the mixture is reduced by two thirds. Add the *DEMI GLACE* and cook for three minutes more. Strain the sauce.

4. Arrange the shrimp over the spinach and pour sauce on top.

MEDALLIONS OF VEAL WITH WILD MUSHROOM SAUCE

1 8-inch section boned veal loin	Salt and fresh black pepper
2 ounces dried morels (or 6 ounces fresh)	2 tablespoons finely chopped shallots
1 1-pound can chanterelles (or 12–ounces fresh)	1 cup dry white wine
12 tablespoons butter	1 cup beef stock (see (recipe on page 166)
	2 cups heavy cream

1. Prepare the veal. Trim off any fat or silvery skin. Slice the loin widthwise into 8 1-inch medallions and pound these lightly with the side of a cleaver.

2. Meanwhile, prepare the mushrooms. If using dried morels, soak them in 2 quarts warm water for 3 hours. Agitate them to wash out any sand, and cut off any dirty stems. If using fresh morels, wash them thoroughly, and cut off the stems. Drain the canned chanterelles and pat dry. If using fresh chanterelles, wash them as described for the morels.

3. Prepare the mushroom sauce. Melt 4 tablespoons butter in a sauté pan over high heat. Add the mushrooms to the pan, sprinkling lightly with salt and pepper. Cook for 1 minute, stirring constantly. Add the shallots, and cook for 1 minute more, stirring constantly. Add the white wine, and bring it to a boil. Add the veal stock, and boil the mixture until only 2 tablespoons liquid remain. Add the

cream and boil the sauce until only 1 cup liquid remains. Correct the seasoning with salt and pepper. The sauce can be made ahead.

4. Just before serving, melt the remaining 8 tablespoons butter in a hot skillet. Season the veal medallions with salt and pepper, and cook them over high heat for 45 seconds per side. Transfer the veal medallions to warm dinner plates, 2 to a plate, and spoon the wild mushrooms sauce on top.

A medallion is a tiny steak cut from the loin. Morels are a wild mushroom distinguished by a conical shape, honeycomb texture, and unusual smoky flavor. Chanterelles are another wild mushroom, orange in color, shaped like a golf tee, and with a peppery taste. At certain times of the year, top green grocers carry both species fresh. Dried morels and canned chanterelles can be found at gourmet shops year 'round.

AMARETTO SOUFFLE

8 egg yolks	2 tablespoons butter
1 cup sugar	8 egg whites
Pinch of salt	¼ teaspoon cream of tartar
1 tablespoon vanilla	½ cup toasted slivered
3 tablespoons cornstarch	almonds
1½ cups milk	AMARETTO SAUCE
¼ cup amaretto	

1. Combine the egg yolks, ¾ cup sugar, salt, and vanilla in a bowl and beat with an electric mixer for 5 minutes, or until the sugar has dissolved. Add the cornstarch and beat for 3 minutes. Meanwhile, bring the milk to a boil, and add it gradually to the yolk mixture. Continue beating for 3 minutes.

2. Transfer the mixture to a heavy saucepan and simmer it over medium heat, whisking vigorously, for 3 minutes, or until thick. Remove the pan from the heat and let the mixture cool. When cool, whisk in the amaretto. Meanwhile, thickly butter the bottom and sides of a 6-cup soufflé dish and sprinkle the inside of the dish with sugar.

3. Beat the egg whites and cream of tartar to stiff peaks, using an electric beater or copper bowl and whisk in the remaining sugar as the whites stiffen. Gently fold the amaretto mixture into the egg whites, using a rubber spatula, gradually sprinkling in the almonds. Spoon the soufflé mixture into the prepared dish, and bake it in a preheated 400° oven for 15-20 minutes. Serve with the *AMARETTO SAUCE* below.

AMARETTO SAUCE

3 egg yolks	1 tablespoon vanilla
½ cup sugar	2 cups heavy cream
2 tablespoons dry white wine	¼ cup confectioner's sugar
	2 tablespoons amaretto

1. Combine the first four ingredients in the top of a double boiler, and cook, whisking constantly, for 3 minutes, or until the mixture thickens. Remove the pan from the heat, continue beating until the mixture is cool, and chill in the refrigerator.

2. Whip the cream to stiff peaks with the confectioner's sugar. Fold the cream into the yolk mixture, followed by the amaretto.

As everyone knows, amaretto is an almond-flavored cordial from Saronno in northern Italy. What you might not know, however, is that the popular liqueur takes its "almond" flavor not from real almonds, but from apricot pits.

Dinner For Six

Salpicon De Marisco Costa Del Sol

Merluza A La Vasca

Cochinillo A La Segoviana

Datilas

Wine:

With the Hake—Marqués de Cáceres White Wine

With the Suckling Pig—Marqués de Cáceres Red Wine

Ted Gould, Owner

Guy Gateau, Mâtre de Cuisine

One of the best Spanish restaurants in Miami is not in Calle Ocho or "Little Havana," but in the ultra-modern Pavillon Hotel. Its name is El Sevilla, and it is the sister restaurant of the prestigious Pavillon Grill.

The Sevilla is decorated with the same refined taste that has made the rest of the hotel a work of art. Pavillon owner Ted Gould flew to Madrid to pick the hand-painted wall tiles and matching dinner plates. The Spanish atmosphere is completed by wrought iron gates, comfortable leather chairs, and strolling guitarist.

Naturally, the Sevilla serves such traditional Spanish dishes as gazpacho, paella, and flan. But you will also find such exotic fare as roast suckling pig and dates stuffed with turron. Sweet-tooths will feel very much at home at the lavish dessert buffet in the middle of the dining room.

The chef at El Sevilla is Adolpho Jimenez, who was born in Malaga, Spain. Presiding over all the Pavillon restaurants is Guy Gateau, one of the most talked about chefs in Miami. "We try to be as authentic as possible." says Gateau of the El Seville. "The only thing that we're missing is a press for making fresh olive oil!"

400 Chopin Plaza

SALPICON DE MARISCO COSTA DEL SOL
Seafood Salad "Costa del Sol"

1 cup white wine
1 pound shrimp, shelled
   and deveined
12 cherrystone clams
½ pound scallops
2 spiny lobster tails
2 potatoes
½ cup freshly shucked peas
   Salt
3 egg yolks
1 tablespoon mustard
1 cup olive oil
2 tablespoons Worchester-
   shire sauce

3 tablespoons ketchup
   Fresh black pepper
1 onion, finely chopped
1 small jar pimentos, diced
5 ounces drained pickles,
   diced
1 head lettuce, broken into
   leaves and washed
1 pound tomatoes, peeled
   seeded, and chopped (see
   page 4)
4 hard-cooked eggs, diced

1. Bring the wine to a gentle simmer and poach the shrimp for 30 seconds, or until cooked. Transfer to a colander to cool. Add the clams to the wine and poach for 2 minutes, or until the shells just open. Transfer to the colander and cool, then remove from the shells. Add the scallops to the wine and poach for 30 seconds, or until cooked. Cool as described above. Poach the lobster tails for 1 minute, or until cooked. Cool as described above and remove the shells. Cut the seafood into ½ inch dice.

2. Peel the potatoes and cut into 1-inch cubes. Place in cold, salted water, bring to a boil, and simmer for 5 minutes, or until the potatoes are cooked. Transfer to the colander to cool. Cook the peas in rapidly boiling, salted water for 30 seconds. Cool in the colander.

3. Prepare the sauce. Place the yolks and mustard in a non-aluminum bowl. Gradually whisk in the olive oil—the sauce should thicken. Whisk in the remaining flavorings—the sauce should be highly seasoned.

4. Mix the diced seafood and vegetables with the sauce. Mix in the onions, pimentos, and pickles. Line one large or six individual salad bowls with lettuce leaves. Spoon in the salad, and garnish with the tomatoes and hard cooked eggs.

This recipe may look involved, but actually it is a series of simple steps. All the seafood can be cooked ahead of time. The salad will, in fact, have more flavor if mixed with the sauce when still warm, and left 5-6 hours in the refrigerator to ripen.

MERLUZA A LA VASCA
(Hake à la Vasca)

2½ pounds hake (or a firm-fleshed white fish)
Salt and fresh black pepper
Juice of 1 lemon
1 cup flour, for dusting (approximate)
4 tablespoons olive oil
1 cup finely chopped onion
3 cloves garlic, finely chopped
1-2 fresh red chili peppers (or to taste), diced
18 medium sliced shrimp, shelled and deveined

12 cherrystone clams, scrubbed
2 tablespoons dry white wine
1 cup bottled clam broth
BECHAMEL SAUCE (see below)
12 asparagus spears
½ cup freshly shucked green peas
3 hard-cooked eggs
3 tablespoons chopped fresh parsley

1. Cut the hake into diagonal, finger-thick slices. Season each slice with salt, pepper, and lemon juice, and lightly dust with flour.

2. Heat the oil in a clay pot and lightly sauté the onion, garlic, and chilis over medium heat. (Do not let brown.) Add the hake and lightly brown the pieces. Add the shrimp, clams, wine, and clam broth. Gently simmer the fish for 10 minutes, shaking the pot to blend the wine and oil.

3. Prepare the *BECHAMEL SAUCE* . Meanwhile, cook the asparagus and peas in rapidly boiling, salted water for 3 minutes, or until tender.

4. To serve: arrange the fish on a platter and spoon the *BECHAMEL SAUCE* on top. Garnish with asparagus spears, peas, chopped hard cooked eggs, and finely chopped parsley.

BECHAMEL SAUCE

2 *tablespoons butter*   1 *cup milk*
2 *tablespoons flour*

1. Melt the butter in a small saucepan. Whisk in the flour and cook over medium heat for 30 seconds. Whisk in the milk and simmer the sauce for 3 minutes. Strain the juices from the fish into the bechamel sauce and whisk until thoroughly mixed.

The Basques are a sturdy and ancient race, who live in the mountains along the French-Spanish border. This dish is traditionally cooked in a clay pot. Pyrex or Corningware will work well, too. Hake is a firm-fleshed white fish; you may, if desired, substitute snapper, halibut, or redfish. The Basques are very fond of chili peppers. To reduce the hotness, you may wish to remove the seeds.

COCHINILLO A LA SEGOVIANA
(Segovian-Style Suckling Pig)

¾ cup finely chopped onion
3 cloves garlic, minced
1 cup dry white wine
3 tablespoons chopped
   fresh parsley
1 teaspoon thyme
3 bay leaves

5 cloves
½ suckling pig (4-6 pounds)
   or 3 large pork tender-
   loins, or a shoulder roast
2 tablespoons oregano
1 tablespoon salt
¼ cup lard

1. Make a marinade by combining the onion, garlic, wine, parsley, thyme, bay leaves, and cloves. Marinate the pork for 4 hours.

2. Remove the pork from the marinade and blot dry. Combine the oregano and salt and rub these into the skin. Smear the lard on top.

3. Preheat the oven to 375°. Place the pig in a roasting pan and roast for 1 hour and 45 minutes, basting frequently with pan juices. If the juice evaporates, add ½ cup water.

The traditional meat for this Segovian specialty is cochinillo *suckling pig In the event that you cannot find suckling pig, this dish can be made with pork tenderloin or shoulder.*

DATILAS
(Dates Stuffed with Turron and Marinated in Brandy)

  1 *bar of* turron
  5 *tablespoons unsalted*
     butter
36 *dried dates*

½ *cup light corn syrup*
½ *cup good cognac*
   Juice of 1 orange

1. Chop the *turron* as finely as possible. Cream the butter and beat in the chopped *turron*. Chill.

2. Pit the dates and place a small piece of *turron* mixture in the center of each.

3. Combine the corn syrup, cognac, and orange juice in a flat saucepan and bring to a boil. Add the dates and gently simmer until warm. Transfer the dates to serving plates. Boil the syrup until thick and spoon it over the dates.

This unusual dessert is made with dates and turron, *a Latin American version of nougat. (You can buy it in Latin American grocery stores.) It is not necessary to uncork a Courvoissier* Paradis, *but try to use a real cognac for the marinade.*

Dinner For Eight

Shrimp Merlin

Scallop Timbale in Basil Sauce

Duckling Jubilee with Cherry Sauce

Spätzle

Blacksmith Pie

Wines:

With the Shrimp — Pouilly Fumé Domaine St. Laurent, 1983

With the Scallops — Chablis, Premier Cru, J. Drouhin, 1983

With the Duck — Puligny Montrachet "Les Folatieres"
Premier Cru, Joseph Drouhin, 1980

David Kurtz, General Manager

Marina Polvay, Food Consultant

THE FORGE

The Forge is the one restaurant that needs no introduction; not to the moguls, movie stars, or Miami's movers and shakers who nightly flock here in their Rolls Royces and limosines. Not to such prestigious organizations as Mobil Travel Guide, Carte Blanche, and Travel/Holiday, which have accorded this Miami Beach institution the highest honors.

Founded in 1930, the Forge is located on the site of a former blacksmith shop. It is hard to believe that this elegant restaurant was once a working smithy. Gone are the dusty coal bins and blazing forge, and in their place are crystal chandeliers, beveled mirrors, and a museum quality collection of Tiffany glass. Gone, too, is the sweaty blacksmith, and in his place stands the dapper general manager, David Kurtz, who reigns over minions of tuxedoed captains and waiters.

But to come to the Forge solely for the sleek brass railings, the velvet walls, the tables set with hand-loomed cloths, pewter service plates, and soft lamp lights would be to overlook a menu designed by a genuine Russian Princess. The arrival of food consultant Marina Polvay revolutionized the Forge's predictable Continental menu, adding *cuisine moderne*—contemporary French cooking.

"Man does not live by bread alone," goes the saying, and oenophiles will find spiritual sustenance here in a cellar that boasts over 30,000 bottles locked behind a solid brass door that once sealed a San Francisco bank vault. The wine list, now in its eighth edition, is as thick as the Miami Yellow Pages. Big spenders will find an 1822 Chateau Lafite Rothschild for $31,000. The rest of us can console ourselves with a collection of California boutique wines unsurpassed in Southern Florida.

432 41st Street
Miami Beach

SHRIMP MERLIN

3 pounds large shrimp
3 quarts water
1 tablespoon thyme
½ teaspoon basil
4 hard-cooked eggs, yolks only
4 tablespoons white wine vinegar
2-3 tablespoons sugar, more to taste

1 teaspoon dry mustard
¼ teaspoon black pepper
1½ cups EASY MAYONNAISE (see below)
4 ounces capers, drained
2 medium onions, sliced into very thin strips
⅓ cup heavy cream, whipped to soft peaks
½ cup sour cream, whisked smooth

1. Shell and devein the shrimp. In a large pot, bring the water to a boil with the thyme and basil. Add the shrimp, and return to a boil. Reduce the heat and simmer for 3-5 minutes, or until the shrimp turn pink. Drain the shrimp and cool completely, discard the poaching liquid.

2. Rub the 4 egg yolks through a sieve into a large bowl. Add vinegar, sugar, mustard, pepper, and *MAYONNAISE*, and blend well. Stir in the capers and onions.

3. Fold in the whipped cream and sour cream, followed by the shrimp. Taste carefully for seasoning; you may wish to add more pepper and a pinch of salt. The taste should be sweet and sour.

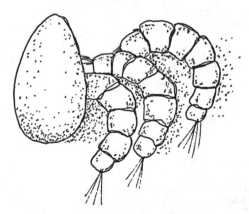

EASY MAYONNAISE

½ teaspoon powdered mustard	Dash cayenne
1 teaspoon water	2 large egg yolks, or 1 large whole egg
½ teaspoon salt, or to taste	2 tablespoons lemon juice
⅛ teaspoon ground white pepper	1 cup salad oil

1. Mix the mustard with the water and allow to steep 5 minutes to develop flavor.

2. Put the mustard in a blender or food processor and mix in the next five ingredients with ¼ cup of the oil. Cover and turn on the motor at high speed. Add the remaining ¾ cup oil in a thin, gradual stream. Turn off the motor and transfer the mayonnaise to a jar. Cover and refrigerate until ready to use.

When making mayonnaise, it is important to have all the ingredients at the same temperature. Add the oil gradually. If the sauce curdles, try adding a few drops of ice water. Makes 1 ½ cups.

SCALLOP TIMBALES IN BASIL SAUCE

1 pound sea scallops	Butter for the timbale molds
2 egg whites	
2 cups heavy cream	8 ¾-cup timbale molds
Salt and white pepper	BASIL SAUCE
A few grains of cayenne pepper	1 cup fresh blueberries
	Fresh basil or mint leaves, for garnish

1. Preheat oven to 400°.

2. Put all ingredients for the scallop mixture into a food processor or blender and blend until smooth and creamy.

3. Butter the timbale or other small molds. Fill the molds to within ½ inch of the top with scallop mixture. Place the molds in the roasting pan and add ½ inch boiling water.

4. Bake 15-20 minutes or until an inserted knife comes out clean. Meanwhile, prepare the sauce.

5. To serve, spoon the sauce onto a platter or individual appetizer plates. Unmold the timbales in the center and garnish with blueberries and mint or basil leaves.

BASIL SAUCE

6 shallots, finely minced	Salt and pepper to taste
2 cups dry white wine	½ tablespoon butter, at
1½ cups heavy cream	room temperature
1 tablespoon fresh minced	⅓ tablespoon flour
basil or ¼ teaspoon dry	
basil	

1. In a saucepan, combine shallots and wine. Bring to a boil, reduce heat, and simmer until reduced by half. Add the cream and seasonings and simmer until reduced by one third. The mixture will be slightly thickened.

2. Mix the butter and flour together to form a thick, smooth paste. Whisk this mixture into the cream mixture and simmer, stirring for 2-3 minutes.

A timbale is a small, cylinder-shaped metal mold. Ramekins or custard cups can be used instead.

DUCKLING JUBILEE

4 *ducks, 4-5 pounds each*
Salt
Juice of 2 lemons

CHERRY SAUCE (see
below)
3 *tablespoons butter*
1 *cup walnut halves*

1. Preheat oven to 450°.

2. Rub ducks inside and outside with salt and lemon juice, and let stand for 5 minutes.

3. Pat the ducks dry. Place them on a rack in a pan deep enough to contain the fat that will melt. (The ducks should not touch; you may need to use several pans.) Put the duck into the preheated oven and roast for 30 minutes.

4. Remove the duck from oven and prick it all over to release some of the fat. Lower the oven temperature to 350°.

5. When the ducks are cool enough to handle, cut them in half lengthwise by cutting between the two breasts and along one side of the back bone.

6. Pour off excess fat from the pan and return ducks to the 350° oven, skin side up. Roast in the oven until brown and crisp, 1 to 1 ½ hours.

7. Remove the ducks from the pan and keep them warm. Make the sauce. Before serving, place ducks under boiler for a few minutes to crisp the skin; do not let it burn. Heat the butter in a skillet, and sauté the walnut halves until golden brown. Garnish the duck with walnuts and serve the sauce on the side.

This method for roasting ducks may seem involved, but it is the only way I know to get rid of the fat.

CHERRY SAUCE

2 cups ruby port
½ cup DEMI-GLACE or
   SAUCE ESPAGNOLE
   (see below)
½ cup kirsch
   Juice of ½ lemon
2-3 tablespoons cornstarch,
   dissolved in 2
   tablespoons of the port

2 cups pitted dark Bing
   cherries, drained, juices
   reserved
¼ teaspoon nutmeg
⅛ teaspoon white pepper
   Salt

1. Pour off duck fat from roasting pan and stir in half of the port to deglaze the pan.

2. In a saucepan, combine the *DEMI-GLACE* or *SAUCE ESPAGNOLE* with the kirsch and the lemon juice. Add the port with deglazed pan juices. Bring to a boil, lower heat, and simmer 5 minutes. The sauce will keep, refrigerated, for one week.

This cherry sauce can be made with either demi-glace *(concentrated beef stock) or* Sauce Espagnole *(a rich meat gravy). You'll find recipes for these sauces on the following pages. You'll find recipes for these sauces on the following pages.*

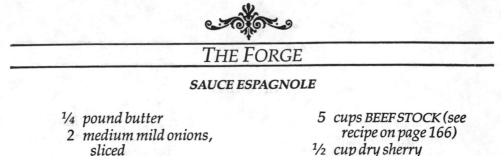

SAUCE ESPAGNOLE

¼ *pound butter*
2 *medium mild onions,*
  sliced
2 *carrots, peeled and thinly*
  sliced
⅓ *cup flour*

5 *cups BEEF STOCK (see*
  recipe on page 166)
½ *cup dry sherry*
½ *cup tomato purée*
  Salt and pepper to taste

1. In a heavy saucepan, heat butter over medium heat and sauté the onions and carrots until brown.
2. Add flour, blend well, and cook over low heat, stirring often, until flour turns golden brown.
3. Add beef stock and sherry, stirring continuously until mixture is well blended.
4. Cover pan and simmer, stirring occasionally, for 1 hour. Add tomato pureé, and salt and pepper. Simmer for 35 minutes.
5. Cool to lukewarm. strain into containers and refrigerate or freeze until ready to use.

Sauce espagnole (literally "Spanish" sauce) is a rich meat gravy.

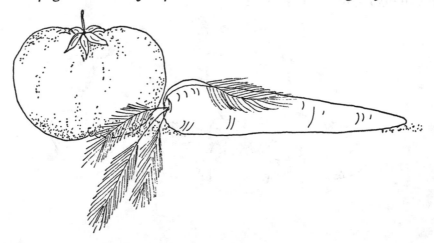

THE FORGE

DEMI-GLACE

6 cups BEEF STOCK (see
   recipe on page 166)

1 tablespoon arrowroot or
   cornstarch
2 tablespoons Madiera

1. Place the stock in a large saucepan and boil it, stirring occasionally, until only 2 cups of liquid remain.
2. Dissolve the arrowroot or cornstarch in Madiera, and whisk this mixture into the reduced stock. Boil the demi-glace for 30 seconds, strain, and cool.

Demi-glace (literally "half glaze") is the secret to smooth, rich, ebony-colored sauces. To make it we boil and reduce beef stock. The process may seem time consuming but the sauce will keep for months in the freezer. Makes 2 cups.

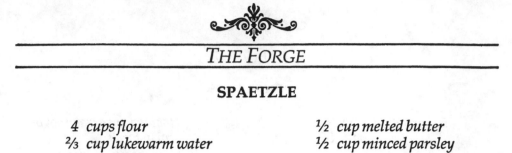

SPAETZLE

4 cups flour	½ cup melted butter
⅔ cup lukewarm water	½ cup minced parsley
4 eggs	Fresh ground pepper
2 tablespoons salt	

1. In a bowl, combine the flour with water, eggs and salt. Beat for at least 3 minutes with a wooden spoon. The dough should be soft, but not runny.

2. Bring a large saucepan of salted water to a boil. Place the dough on a wet board. Use a knife to cut ½ inch pieces into the boiling water. Reduce heat to medium and cook until noodles rise to the top.

3. Drain well. Serve with butter, parsley and freshly ground pepper.

Spaetzle are tiny dumplings. You can use a knife to cut them or buy a special spaetzle cutter.

BLACKSMITH PIE

FOR THE CRUST:

10 ounces graham crackers
10 ounces Pepperidge Farm Fudge Cookies
½ cup melted butter

FOR THE VANILLA PUDDING:

4 tablespoons cornstarch
3 tablespoons VANILLA SUGAR (see below)
Pinch of salt
2 cups light cream
1 envelope unflavored gelatin

⅓ cup cold water
1 whole egg
2 egg yolks (reserve the whites for the custard)
1 tablespoon butter

TO FINISH THE FILLING:

12 ounces semisweet chocolate
3½ cups heavy cream
1½ cups powdered sugar
2 egg whites
½ teaspoon vanilla extract
1 ounce chocolate, for garnish

1. Prepare the crust. Crush the crackers and cookies to fine crumbs in a food processor or with a rolling pin. Mix the crumbs with the butter and press the dough into a 10-inch pie pan. Chill for one hour.

2. Prepare the pudding. Combine the cornstarch, *VANILLA SUGAR* and salt in a saucepan. Gradually add the cream, stirring until smooth. Cook the mixture over low heat for 5 minutes, or until thick. Meanwhile, soften the gelatin over the water in a metal measuring cup. Place the cup in a shallow pan of simmering water until the gelatin is completely melted. Whisk it into the pudding. Remove the pan from the heat. Beat the eggs with the yolks and whisk them into the hot pudding mixture. Dot the top with butter, cool to room temperature, then chill.

3. Prepare the chocolate mixture. Melt the chocolate over a double boiler and mix it with 1 cup of the cooled pudding mixture. Beat the cream with 1 cup powdered sugar to stiff peaks. Fold ⅔ of the whipped cream into the chocolate mixture, and spread it over the bottom of the crust. Chill for 10 minutes.

4. Prepare the custard mixture. Fold 1 cup whipped cream into the remaining vanilla pudding. Beat the egg whites to stiff peaks, sprinkling in the remaining ½ cup sugar and vanilla at the end. Fold the whites into the pudding mixture and spoon it into the pie shell. Chill for 1 hour. Before serving, frost the pie with the remaining whipped cream and decorate with chocolate shavings. (Use a sharp paring knife or vegetable peeler to shave the chocolate.)

VANILLA SUGAR

3 cups granulated sugar   *2 whole vanilla beans, split*

Combine the sugar and vanilla beans in a jar with a tight lid for at least three days. The vanilla flavor will be much more pleasing than that obtained with vanilla extract.

Dinner For Six

She Crab Soup

Escargots with Rosemary

Beef Tenderloin "Grand Chateau"

Délices de Fraise et des Framboises "Grand Cafe"

Wines:

With the soup and Escargots—Callaway Chenin Blanc, 1981

With the Beef—Amarone Sartori, 1979

Bradley Weiser, Assistant General Manager

Edward Steiner, Restaurant Manager

Who says hotel dining is just for the tourists? "That went out with the American plan," says Brad Weiser, assistant general manager and son of the owner of the Grand Bay Hotel. Not only is the Grand Bay one of Miami's most popular meeting places—it also attracts the world's most glittering stars. Michael Jackson, Elton John, Jane Fonda, Luciano Pavarotti, Prince, and Ted Kennedy are but a few of the guests who have recently stayed at the Grand Bay.

The hotel has a restaurant, the Grand Café. The Café is the home of she crab soup and black linguini (made with squid ink)—both winners for two years in a row at the Taste of the Grove food festival. The menu, drawn by artist Fred Albert, reflects the kitchen's fondness for nouvelle cuisine. Among the more innovative culinary creations here are cream of brie soup, basil gnocchi, and lobster with tomato fettuccine.

The Café is decorated in the rich European style that characterizes the rest of the hotel. The ceilings are mirrored and stained glass; there are miles of brass railings; and fresh cut flowers bloom everywhere. The tables are set with pale pink tablecloths and crowned with flickering candles.

The Grand Bay Hotel has 188 hotel rooms. The best night's sleep is to be had in one of the eight international suites. Each suite has a theme—French, English, American, Italian, Moroccan, African, Chinese, and South American—and all have private balconies, spiral staircases, and sunken baths. Not a bad place to curl up after a meal at the Grand Café. Not a bad place at all.

2669 South Bayshore Drive
Coconut Grove

SHE CRAB SOUP

2 tablespoons finely chopped shallots	4 cups bottled clam broth
⅓ cup sherry	2 cups heavy cream
1½ pounds lump crab meat	2 teaspoons cornstarch
3 tablespoons paprika	½ teaspoon cayenne pepper
2 pinches thyme	Salt and fresh black pepper, to taste

1. Combine the shallots and sherry in a large saucepan and simmer until reduced by half. Add the crab, paprika, and thyme, and simmer for 3 minutes. Add the clam broth and cream, and bring the soup to a boil.

2. Dissolve the cornstarch in 1 teaspoon water and whisk it into the soup. Simmer for five minutes, adding the seasonings to taste.

This soup tastes best made with backfin lump meat from a female crab, whence the name. The best paprika is imported from Hungary and should be stored in the freezer once opened. Clam broth is widely sold bottled. The soup will be even better if you reserve the broth from freshly steamed clams.

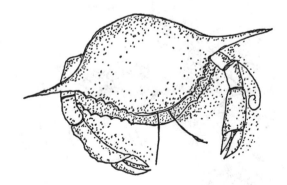

ESCARGOTS WITH ROSEMARY

36 large snails
2 sticks (1 cup) unsalted
   butter, at room
   temperature
1½ tablespoons finely
   chopped, fresh rosemary

Salt and fresh black pepper
⅓ cup dry white wine
⅓ tablespoon cognac
French bread

1. Rinse the escargots and blot dry. Cream the butter and beat in the herbs and seasonings.

2. Arrange the escargots in 6 small ramekins or casserole dishes. Spread the herbed butter on top and sprinkle the snails with wine and cognac.

3. Just before serving, bake the snails in a preheated 450° oven for 5 minutes or until the butter is melted and bubbling. Serve the escargots at once, with plenty of French bread for dipping.

Escargots are French land snails—conveniently sold by the can (with or without shells). In this recipe, the snails are baked in small ramekins. It is essential to use fresh rosemary.

BEEF TENDERLOIN "GRAND CHATEAU"

1 *beef tenderloin (3 pounds trimmed)*
1½ *bottles dry red wine*
5 *tablespoons finely chopped shallots*

7 *tablespoons butter*
¾ *cup DEMI GLACE SAUCE (see recipe on page 55)*
Salt and fresh black pepper
4 *tablespoons oil*

1. Trim all sinew and fat off the tenderloin. Cut it into 12 1-inch slices, which are called medallions.

2. Meanwhile, prepare the sauce. Melt 3 tablespoons butter in a wide saucepan and sauté the shallots over medium heat for 30 seconds, or until soft but not browned. Add the wine, and increase the heat to high. Boil the wine until ¾ cup liquid remains. Whisk in the *DEMI-GLAZE SAUCE.* Correct the seasoning.

3. Just before serving, heat 4 tablespoons butter and the oil in a skillet. Season the beef medallions on both sides and sauté over high heat for 1 minute per side, or until cooked to taste.

4. To serve, place two beef medallions on each plate and top with sauce. If desired, arrange baby vegetables on the side.

The red wine sauce can be made with dry red wine from Bordeaux or a good cabernet sauvignon from California. As an accompaniment to the beef, we suggest boiled baby vegetables quickly sautéed in butter.

DELICES DES FRAISES ET DES FRAMBOISES "GRAND CAFE"
(Strawberry and Raspberry Delight "Grand Café")

1 pound fresh strawberries	⅔ cup light cream
½ cup sugar (or to taste)	1 pound fresh raspberries
2 tablespoons vanilla	1 pint strawberry ice cream
½ cup triple sec	12 fresh mint leaves

1. Pick through the berries. Combine half the strawberries, half the sugar, half the vanilla, half the triple sec, and ⅓ cup cream in a blender. Purée until smooth and chill the sauce until serving. Rinse the blender.

2. Combine half the raspberries with the remaining sugar, vanilla, and triple sec in the blender, and purée until smooth. Chill until serving. Whip the remaining ⅓ cup cream to stiff peaks.

3. To serve, pour a spoonful of strawberry sauce on the bottom half of each of 6 chilled dessert plates. Pour an equal amount of the raspberry sauce on the top half. The sauces should meet in the center and each plate should be completely covered. Neatly place a scoop of strawberry ice cream in the center of each plate. Garnish each plate with the remaining berries. Pipe a rosette of cream on top of each plate and decorate with fresh mint leaves.

This dish was invented by Edward Steiner, former owner of L'Alouette restaurant.

RISTORANTE Il TULIPANO

Dinner For Six

Agnolotti Bandiera with Three Sauces

Shrimp Pancettati in Salsa-Verde with Risotto

Vitello Mandorlato

Zabaglione

Wines:

With the Shrimp — Greco di Tufo

With the Veal — Taurasi Riserva, 1977

With the Zabaglione — Asti Spumante

Filippo Il Grande, Owner

IL TULIPANO

President of the *Societa del Buon Gustai* (Society of Good Taste). Chairman of the Sommelier Guild. Conseiller Culinaire of the prestigious *Confrerie de la Chaine des Rotisseurs*. I'm talking about Filippo Il Grande, owner of the Il Tulipano restaurant in North Miami.

Filippo comes from Tropea, Italy, on the Tyrrhenian Sea. One of ten children, he left home at the age of thirteen to attend hotel school in Bardonecchia, in the Italian Alps. He speaks three languages fluently (Italian, French and English) and says he has his father to thank for that.

Filippo, along with his soft-spoken chef Sandrino, will do just about anything to "entertain the palate," including keeping a list of customers' favorite dishes, so he can call when they are being served. "We use as many native Italian products as possible," says Filippo, "to bring our customers as close to Italy as we can."

This 64-seat restaurant specializes in Northern Italian cuisine. Among the many outstanding dishes here are *Agnolotti Impannate* (pasta rounds stuffed with spinach and served with three sauces), *Pollo Scarpariello* (chicken with Italian sausages and olives), and an ethereal *Zabaglione*.

Filippo brings to his restaurant an extensive background in wine. Before opening Il Tulipano, he served as cellar master at the Jockey Club and Turnberry Isle. He was also featured on Alexander's Vineyards, a television show on wine tasting. But the real secret of Il Tulipano is the dedicated waiter staff. "They don't forget you after you have paid your bill," Filippo says.

11052 Biscayne Boulevard

AGNOLOTTI BANDIERA WITH THREE SAUCES
(Spinach–Filled Pasta with Three Sauces)

2 cups flour, plus flour
   for dusting
½ teaspoon salt
½ teaspoon white pepper
1 stick unsalted butter,
   cut into pieces
4 eggs
1 egg beaten with a pinch of
   salt for egg wash
   Semolina for sprinkling

   FOR THE FILLING:
¼ pound fresh spinach
3 ounces mortadella
   (an Italian cold cut)

3 ounces top quality
   cooked ham
3 ounces ricotta cheese
1 tablespoon Parmesan
   cheese
1 tablespoon olive oil
   Salt and fresh black
   pepper
   PANNA (Traditional
   Cream Sauce)
   FILETTO DI POMODORO
   (Tomato Sauce)
   PESTO ALLA GENOVESE
   (Pesto Sauce)

1. Prepare the pasta. Place the dry ingredients and butter in a food processor fitted with a pastry blade and run the machine for 1 minute, or until the butter is cut up and the mixture feels sandy. Add the eggs and run the machine in quick spurts for 2 minutes, or until the dough forms a compact ball.

2. Cut the dough into four or five small pieces. Lightly flour each and roll it through the pasta machine (set rollers at widest gap). When the dough is smooth, reduce the gap between the rollers and roll the dough again. Continue in this fashion until the rollers are at their narrowest setting. As the dough sheets come out, dust them lightly with flour and spread them out on the table.

3. Prepare the filling. Steam the spinach for 30 seconds or until tender, rinse it under cold water, and squeeze it tightly to extract all the water. Place the spinach and remaining ingredients for the filling in the food processor and grind until smooth.

4. Fill and shape the *agnolotti*: Brush one sheet of pasta dough with the egg glaze. Spoon the filling into a pastry bag (fitted with a ¼ inch round tip). Pipe walnut-sized mounds of filling onto the pasta, leaving 2 inches between each mound. Lay a second sheet of pasta on

top. Gently press the top sheet around the mounds of filling with your fingers. Use an *agnolotti* cutter or 2-inch round cookie cutter to cut out individual circles. Repeat until all the pasta and filling are used up. You should wind up with approximately 36 pieces. Sprinkle each piece with semolina. Keep chilled until ready to cook. Meanwhile, prepare the sauces.

5. Cook the *agnolotti* in rapidly boiling, lightly salted water for 3 minutes, or until they rise back to the surface. Place three *agnolotti* on each plate. Spoon cream sauce over one, red sauce over the second, and green pesto sauce over the third.

PANNA
(Traditional Cream Sauce)

1 cup heavy cream	3 tablespoons freshly grated
1 stick unsalted butter,	Parmesan cheese
cut into pieces	
Salt, white pepper,	
freshly grated nutmeg	

1. Bring the cream to a boil in a large saucepan, stirring to keep it from boiling over. Simmer until the volume of cream has reduced by ⅓.

2. Whisk in the butter, followed by the seasonings, and gently simmer for 2 minutes. Whisk in the cheese.

Do not let the sauce boil too much or overcook, or it will curdle.

FILETTO DI POMODORO
(Fresh Tomato Sauce)

2 medium-sized beefsteak	3 cloves garlic, finely
tomatoes	chopped
4 cups imported canned	Salt and fresh black pepper
plum tomatoes	3 tablespoons finely
¾ cup olive oil	chopped fresh basil
1 cup finely chopped	
Spanish red onion	

1. Peel and seed the tomatoes. Cut a small X on the bottom of the beefsteak tomatoes and cut out the stem ends. Plunge the tomatoes in boiling water for 15 seconds, rinse under cold water, and pull off the skins. Cut the tomatoes in half widthwise and squeeze them, cut side down, in the palms of your hands to wring out the seeds. Cut the tomatoes into thin slivers. Seed the canned tomatoes the same way. Strain the can juices (to remove seeds) and reserve.

2. Heat the olive oil in a large saucepan and cook the onions and garlic over medium heat until golden brown. Add the reserved tomato juice, and boil for 2 minutes. Add the tomatoes and simmer for 3 minutes. Season the sauce with salt and pepper to taste. Just before serving, sprinkle the tomato sauce with fresh basil.

PESTO ALLA GENOVESE
(Pesto Sauce)

2 cups fresh sweet basil	1 cup Italian olive oil
½ cup fresh parsley	¾ cup vegetable oil
4 tablespoons pine nuts (pignoli)	3 tablespoons Parmesan cheese
2 cloves garlic	Salt and white pepper

1. Place all ingredients in a food processor with a steel blade and grind until the mixture forms into a smooth paste.

2. Place the mixture in a small sauce pan and warm quickly over medium heat.

   It is imperative to use fresh basil when making pesto. This recipe comes from Genoa on the Ligurian coast.

SHRIMP PANCETTATI IN SALSA-VERDE WITH RISOTTO

18 jumbo shrimp	4 tablespoons olive oil
18 thin slices of pancetta	6 small bamboo skewers
Salt and pepper to taste	SALSA VERDE
½ cup flour for dusting (approximately)	RISOTTO

1. Prepare the *GREEN SAUCE* and *RISOTTO* (see below).

2. Peel and devein the shrimp. Wrap each shrimp with a slice of pancetta. Lightly season with salt and pepper and dust with flour. Thread the shrimp on skewers, three to a skewer.

3. Heat the olive oil in a large frying pan and sauté the shrimp for a few seconds on each side. Cook the shrimp in a preheated 350° oven for 2-3 minutes.

4. To finish the dish, spoon the rice onto six warm plates. Remove the skewers from the shrimp and arrange three shrimp on each plate. Pour the green sauce on the shrimp and serve at once.

Pancetta is Italian bacon made by curing belly pork.

SALSA VERDE
Green Sauce

½ pound unsalted butter (at room temperature)	Salt and pepper
1 bunch fresh parsley, washed, dried, and stems removed	½ cup heavy cream

1. Place all ingredients except the cream in a food processor and process until the parsley is finely chopped and ingredients are well blended. Place the mixture in a bowl and freeze for ten minutes.

2. Bring the cream to a boil in a shallow pan. Whisk in the herb butter little by little until the sauce is creamy and foamy.

There are two kinds of parsley, curley leaf and flat leaf. I prefer the flat leaf because it has more flavor.

RISOTTO
Italian Rice

2 cups short grain rice	3 cups chicken stock
1 stick butter	Salt and pepper to taste
1 cup finely chopped onions	½ cup freshly grated
¼ pound fresh mushrooms, washed and quartered (about one cup)	Parmesan cheese

1. Melt the butter in a large saucepan over high heat and sauté the onions and mushrooms for 3 minutes or until the onions are soft and golden. Stir in the rice and cook for 1 minute. Add the chicken stock one cup at a time. Bring to a boil and simmer uncovered for 15 minutes, or until the rice is soft and the liquid is completely absorbed. Add salt and pepper to taste. Press a piece of buttered foil over the rice to keep it warm until ready to use.

2. At serving time, sprinkle the grated Parmesan cheese over the rice and toss gently.

The secret to this recipe is using genuine Italian long-grained rice. My favorite brand is Arborio, grown in Piemonte, but any imported Italian brand will do.

VITELLO MANDORLATO
(Stuffed Veal with Almonds)

6 veal cutlets

FOR THE STUFFING:

⅓ pound mozzarella
  cheese, grated
⅓ pound prosciutto or
  Parma ham, diced
1 egg yolk
1 tablespoon finely
  chopped parsley
2 tablespoons freshly
  grated Parmesan
  cheese
  Salt and fresh black
  pepper

FOR THE VEAL:

½ cup flour
2 eggs beaten
½ cup slivered almonds
½ cup fresh bread crumbs
4 tablespoons olive oil
6 thin slices mozzarella
  cheese

TO FINISH THE DISH:

½ bottle dry red wine
3 cups DEMI–GLACE
1 cup washed, quartered
  fresh mushrooms
  Salt and pepper
1½ pounds spinach,
  stemmed, washed and
  steamed

1. Pound the veal with the side of a cleaver between two sheets of dampened waxed paper. This tenderizes the veal. Combine the ingredients for the stuffing, seasoning to taste. Place a spoonful of stuffing on each veal cutlet, fold in half, and secure the ends with a toothpick. Preheat the oven to 350°.

2. For the veal: dip each stuffed cutlet first in flour, then in egg, then finally in the almonds and bread crumbs. Heat the olive oil in a heavy frying pan and brown the veal cutlets quickly on all sides. Transfer the veal with a slotted spoon to a baking dish, and place a slice of mozzarella on top of each. Bake the veal for 10 minutes.

3. To make the sauce: place the wine in a large saucepan and boil until only ½ cup liquid remains. Add the *DEMI–GLACE* and mushrooms, and simmer for 3 minutes. Season to taste with salt and pepper.

4. To finish the dish place each stuffed cutlet in the center of a warm dinner plate. Surround with spinach and ladle the sauce over the veal.

ZABAGLIONE

9 egg yolks
1 cup sweet Marsala wine
½ cup dry white wine
½ tablespoons sugar
1½ cups heavy whipping
   cream

1 pint strawberries,
  blueberries, or
  raspberries

1. Put first four ingredients in a double boiler over gentle simmering water and whisk for 5 minutes, or until the sauce is frothy and thick enough to leave a ribbon trail. Let cool slightly.

2. Whip the heavy cream in a copper bowl or electric mixer to stiff peaks.

3. Working over a bowl of ice, fold the whipped cream into the egg mixture and gently spoon it into serving dishes. Garnish with fresh berries.

Do not overcook the sauce or it will curdle. Refrigerate it until ready to serve.

This frothy Italian egg desert has a curious history. It is named for one Marechal Balione, who defended Florence against the Castracani in the 15th century. Reduced to eggs and brandy (the enemy having captured the provision wagon), the Marshal's chef invented a sweet dessert, which he called zuppa baglioni—"Baglioni's soup." In time the term was shortened to zabaglione (pronounced "za-by-own-e").

Joe's

Stone Crab Restaurant

Dinner For Six

Stone Crabs with Mustard Sauce

Cottage Fried Sweet Potatoes

Grilled Tomatoes

Apple Pie

Wine:

With the Stone Crabs — Mirassou Dry Chablis

JoAnn and Irwin Sawitz, Owners

JOE'S STONE CRAB

T he most powerful man on Miami Beach is neither the mayor, the banker, nor the real estate developer. Rather it is the maître d' of the legendary Joe's Stone Crab. It is he who decides which of the hundreds of guests who line up here nightly gain quick access and which will wait up to an hour and a half for a table.

Joe's seats some 400 people in three sprawling dining rooms. The newest room, the Garden Room, has the old Florida charm of tiled floors, whirling paddle fans, and a view of a plant-filled courtyard. The atmosphere is noisy and boisterous, but not without a certain elegance.

As the name suggests, stone crabs are the house specialty. The mustard sauce served with the crab is a delicacy in itself. Other house specialties include coleslaw, crispy homefries, and a key lime pie that has set a state wide standard.

It is common knowledge that Joe Weiss Sr. came here from New York in 1913 to open a tiny sandwich shop. It was not until 1923, however, that Joe discovered the Florida stone crab, insuring the success of the restaurant for four generations.

Joe's son Jesse took charge of the restaurant in the 30s. Jesse can still be found sitting at the family table, telling tales of Joe's in the old days. Asked why the car in the giant photo hanging in the dining room is called the "Mayflower," for example, Jesse replied "because many women came across in it."

Jesse has a daughter named JoAnn, who married her high school sweetheart, Irwin. This brings us to the third genertion of Joe's. Say, as Irwin is affectionately called, has no funny stories, but he can tell you how he installed computers and how he ships stone crabs to Osaka Joe's and Tokyo Joe's. JoAnn can tell you how her son, Steve, is being groomed for the fourth generation.

When asked, "Say, what makes these stone crabs better than anyone else's?" "I don't know," he replied with a straight face. "I don't eat them anywhere else!"

227 Biscayne St., Miami Beach

STONE CRABS

Fresh stone crab claws
(5 claws — 1½
pounds per person)
Ice

Lemon wedges
Hot melted butter
MUSTARD SAUCE

1. Store the crabs in ice until ready to serve.
2. To crack the claws for serving, place them on a cutting board and cover with a cloth. Crack the shell with a wide-headed mallet, starting at the knuckle, working toward the claw.
3. Pile the claws in a pyramid shape on a platter. Garnish with lemon wedges and serve with hot melted butter or *MUSTARD SAUCE*.

The stone crab wasn't very popular until Joe Sr. had the idea to serve it chilled—which firms up the flesh. Today Joe's has 40 boats that bring in one ton of stone crabs a day. The fishermen use only the male crab, removing the claws, and throwing the bodies back in the water. In a mere six weeks, the crab will grow a usable claw again.

MUSTARD SAUCE

3½ teaspoons Coleman's
dry English mustard
1 cup mayonnaise
2 teaspoons Worcestershire
sauce

1 teaspoon A-1 sauce
2 tablespoons light cream
⅛ teaspoon Salt

Combine the mustard and mayonnaise in a bowl and beat for 1 minute. Add the remaining ingredients and beat until the mixture is smooth and creamy.

Much imitated, never duplicated, this mustard sauce is almost as famous as the stone crabs themselves. Makes 1½ cups.

COTTAGE FRIED SWEET POTATOES

4 *sweet potatoes*
1 *quart vegetable oil, for*
frying

Salt

1. Cut the sweet potatoes into slices as thin as potato chips. Soak them in ice water until you are ready to serve them.

2. At the last minute, heat the oil in a fryer or electric frying pan to 400°. Blot the sweet potato slices dry and fry them for 2 minutes, or until crisp and golden-brown. Remove the chips with a slotted spoon and drain on paper towels. Sprinkle with salt and serve at once.

We use a tool called a mandoline for slicing the potatoes. A mandoline looks like an expensive Vege-matic. You could also use the slicing blade of a food processor.

GRILLED TOMATOES

4 *beefsteak tomatoes*
   oil, for the baking sheet
2 *cups CREAMED SPINACH*
   (use your favorite recipe
   or the recipe on page 108)

3 *cups seasoned bread crumbs*
¾ *cup melted butter*
   Salt and pepper
1½ *cups grated mild cheddar*
   cheese

1. Cut each tomato into 3 thick slices and arrange these on an oiled baking sheet.

2. Prepare the filling. Combine the *CREAMED SPINACH* with the seasoned bread crumbs, melted butter, salt, and pepper. The mixture should be very thick. Spread each tomato slice with the spinach mixture and sprinkle with grated cheese.

3. Just before serving, place the tomatoes under the broiler, and cook until the cheese is melted and golden-brown.

APPLE PIE

CRUST:

2 cups flour
½ teaspoon sugar
⅛ teaspoon salt
½ cup lard
½ cup ice water

1 egg, beaten, for glaze

FILLING:

4 cups canned apples
(our favorite brand is
White House)
¼ teaspoon cinnamon
¼ teaspoon nutmeg
3 tablespoons butter
1 cup sugar

1. Prepare the crust. Combine the flour, sugar, and salt in a bowl. Cut in the lard with two knives or a pastry cutter. The mixture should be smooth and crumbly. Slowly work in the ice water and knead the dough until smooth. Roll the dough into a bowl and dust with flour. Cover it with plastic wrap and refrigerate for 1 hour.

2. Roll out half the dough and use it to line a 9-inch pie pan. Brush the inside of this crust with beaten egg.

3. Prepare the filling. Combine the apples with the spices. Pour the apples into the crust and top with the butter and sugar. Roll out the remaining dough and place it on top of the pie. Prick the top crust with a fork and brush it with the remaining beaten egg.

4. Bake the pie in a preheated 350° oven for 1 hour, or until well browned.

Apple pie was the first dessert on Joe's menu. As the owners refuse to part with the recipe for the famous key lime pie, we hope you'll be consoled with this one.

La Scala Restaurant

Dinner For Four

Paglia E Fieno

Filet Di Dentice Alla Casalinga

Veal Francese

Oranges Alla Cleopatra

Wines:

With the Pasta — Pinot Grigio, 1982

With the Fish — Barolo, 1980

With Desert — Moscato

Giuseppe Pichler, Owner

Mario Cortonesi, Owner

Morella Valentini, Owner

LA SCALA

To Italians, La Scala is a magnificent Opera House in Milan. To Miamians, La Scala is a cozy Italian restaurant on Key Biscayne at the L'Esplanade Mall.

You couldn't ask for an Italian restaurant with a more elegant atmosphere. High hat lights cast a soft glow; rich green wallpaper decks the walls; every table is graced by a single red rose. And what Italian restaurant would be complete without travel posters.

What makes La Scala tick are three partners: Giuseppe Pichler, Mario Cortonesi, and Morella Valentini. Giuseppe runs the back of the restaurant, leaving the dining room to the dashing Mario. The third partner, Morella, makes sure the other two don't get out of hand. (Morella is Mario's wife!) "We could not have done this without Morella," says Giuseppe. "She believed in us and supported us all the way." So even though you do not see Morella at the restaurant, she is very much an integral part of La Scala's success.

Mario and Giuseppe both attended hotel school in Italy before joining Royal Caribbean Cruise Line. Giuseppe likes his new home in the United States. "I am grateful to be in the United States," he says. "In Italy, I would not have had the opportunity to open a restaurant of my own." Giuseppe loves the Latin influence in Miami. "It creates a European feeling," he says.

Begin your meal with antipasti from a trolly from which nothing has been left out. The selection includes mortadella, roasted peppers, seafood salad, ceviche, olives, zucchini, eggplant in tomato sauce, tomatoes and mozzarella, and mushrooms in wine. In the unlikely event you find nothing on the menu that appeals to you, the chef will be happy to prepare whatever you want.

L'Esplanade Mall
Key Biscayne

PAGLIA E FIENO
(White and Green Linguine with Vegetables and Ham)

4 tablespoons butter
1½ cups fresh mushrooms, chopped
½ cup cooked ham, chopped
Salt and pepper
2 cups heavy or whipping cream

¼ pound thin white linguine
¼ pound thin green linguine
½ cup fresh grated Parmesan cheese
1 egg yolk
Chopped parsley, for garnish

1. Melt the butter and sauté the mushrooms and ham until the mushrooms are tender, about 5 minutes. Season with salt and pepper. Add the cream and bring to a boil. Reduce the heat and simmer for 2 minutes.

2. Bring a large pot of salted water to a boil. Add the pasta and cook until "firm to the tooth," *al dente*, about 8 minutes. Drain well and add the pasta to the sauce.

3. Add the cheese and egg yolk and stir thoroughly. Garnish with chopped parsley and serve at once.

Pasta should be slightly chewy. In Italy we say al dente, *literally, "cooked to the tooth."*

The name of this dish literally means "straw and hay," referring to the two hues of pasta.

FILET DI DENTICE ALLA CASALINGA
(Snapper with Shrimp and Vegetables)

¼ cup olive oil, more if
    necessary
1 small onion, sliced
1 pound fillet of snapper,
    cut into 4 pieces
½ cup flour
2 garlic cloves, crushed
4 medium shrimp

2 cups mushrooms, sliced
1 cup dry white wine
6 tomatoes, peeled, seeded
    and chopped (see
    instructions on page 4)
Salt and pepper
Chopped parsley for
    garnish

1. In a large frying pan, heat the oil over medium heat and sauté the onions for 5 minutes.

2. Sprinkle the snapper fillets with flour. Add garlic to the pan and then the fillets. Brown the fillets on both sides.

3. Add the shrimp and mushrooms and sauté for 30 seconds. Add the wine and let it simmer for 1 minute. Add the tomatoes and simmer for another few minutes or until the fish is tender and flakes easily with a fork. Season the sauce to taste with salt and pepper. Sprinkle the fish with parsley, and serve at once. Boiled potatoes would make a fine accompaniment.

VEAL FRANCESE

12 veal scallopine, pounded thin	½ pound fresh mushrooms, sliced
1 cup flour	1 cup dry white wine
3 eggs, lightly beaten	Juice of 2 lemons
¾ cup olive oil, more if necessary	Salt and pepper
1 stick butter	Chopped parsley for garnish

1. Sprinkle the veal with flour and then dip into beaten eggs.

2. In a large frying pan, heat the oil over a medium heat. Add as many veal slices as you can without having them touch each other and cook for 5 minutes, turning once, or until the scallopines are lightly browned and the veal is cooked. Repeat with the rest of the veal. Transfer the veal to a platter and keep warm.

3. Discard the oil from the pan. Add the butter and mushrooms. Sauté for 5 minutes, or until the mushrooms are tender.

4. Add wine and lemon juice and simmer for a few more minutes to reduce the sauce. Season with salt and pepper. Spoon the sauce over the veal and garnish with chopped parsley. Serve at once.

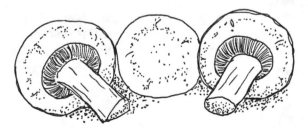

ORANGES ALLA CLEOPATRA

4 oranges   2 cups water
1 cup sugar   1 cup Grand Marnier

1. Remove 2 inch strips of "zest" from the oranges. Be sure to remove the zest only and not the bitter white pith. Cut the strips of zest lengthwise into very fine slivers. Bring a small saucepan of water to boil, add the zest, and simmer for 1 minute to remove the bitterness. Drain.

2. Using a sharp knife, carve the white pitch away from the oranges so that only the orange flesh remains. Place the oranges in a glass bowl.

3. In a heavy saucepan melt the sugar with 1 cup of the water over low heat, stirring occasionally until it is clear. Use a wet pastry brush to dissolve any crystals that form inside the pan. Boil the syrup, without stirring, until it begins to brown. Remove from the heat at once; the syrup will continue to cook for a few seconds once it has begun to carmelize.

4. Add the remaining cup of water all at once and stand back quickly. *(It will sputter and hiss like Vesuvius.)* Return the pan to the heat and simmer the syrup, stirring, until reduced by half.

5. Add Grand Marnier and orange zest to the syrup. Marinate the oranges in this mixture in the refrigerator for 24 hours.

6. To serve, slice oranges crosswise and cover with sauce and julienned orange zest.

The zest is the oil-rich outer rind of the orange. It is best removed with a vegetable peeler. You want to avoid the white pith underneath, which is bitter.

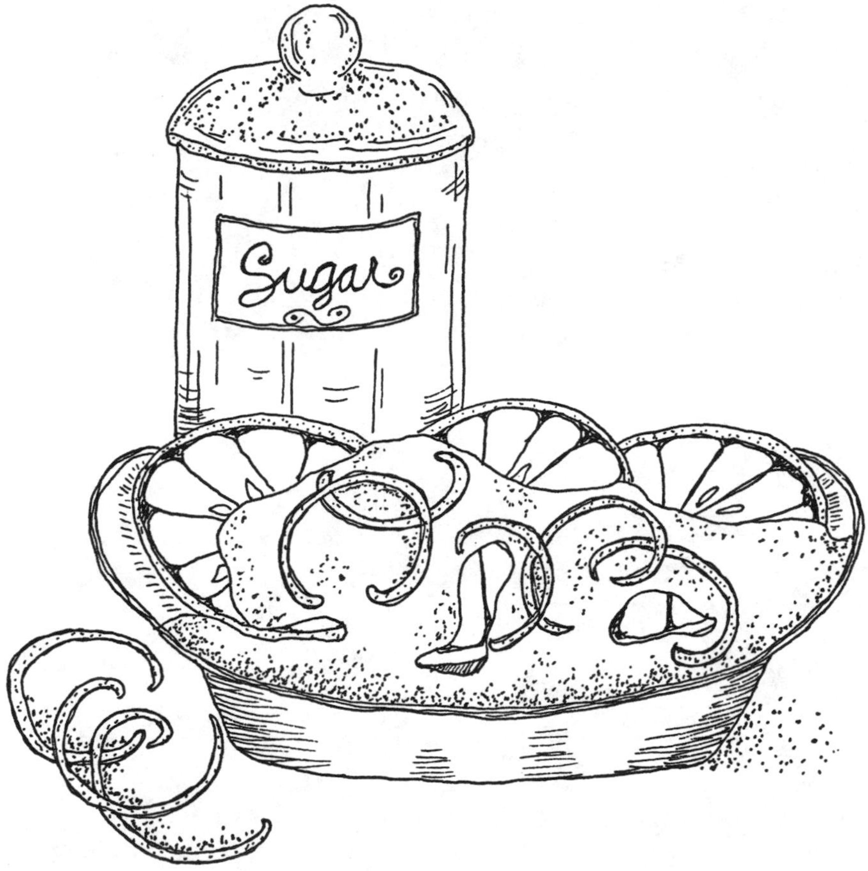
Sugar

Le Festival

Dinner For Four

Le Salade Monte Carlo

Le Filet de Red Snapper Duglere

Le Carré d'Agneau Bouquetière

Soufflé au Grand Marnier with Sabayon Sauce

Wines:

With the Snapper — Puligny-Montrachet, 1979

With the Lamb — Chateau Beychevelle, 1975

Jacque Baudean, Owner

Jean Paul Robin, Owner and Chef

From the fish-rich province of Brittany and the wine capital of Bordeaux come Jean-Paul Robin and Jacques Baudean, owners of the fashionable Le Festival. Founded in 1976, this French restuarant is housed in an old clothing warehouse in the heart of Coral Gables.

It did not take long for Le Festival to catch on. Within six months, it had received rave reviews from the Miami Herald, and within a year, it was awarded the coveted Cartier "Golden Spoon" and Travel/Holiday Magazine Fine Dining Award.

Jean-Paul got his start on the luxury liner S.S. France, working as chef for the officers' kitchen. It was there that he met Jacques Baudean, who would become his partner and lifelong friend. On a port of call to Cannes, Jean-Paul saw a sign for the Cannes Film Festival, and knew that if he ever had a restaurant, he would call it *Le Festival*.

"When you Americans landed on the moon, I arrived in New York," recalls the soft-spoken chef. The next stop was a two year stint at the renowned Café Chauveron before Jean-Paul joined forces with Jacques to open a restaurant of their own: Le Festival.

Le Festival serves classical French cuisine. Among the many dishes you will find on its oversized menu are *crêpes de fruits de mer* (seafood crêpes), *Caneton à l'orange* (roast Long Island duckling with orange sauce, and *soufflé au Grand Marnier* (Grand Marnier soufflé). The restaurant is equally famous for its *pommes chatouillards*, literally "tickling potatoes"—which Jean-Paul affectionately calls "French fries."

Le Festival is a pretty restaurant, whose red and white-striped walls are decked with art nouveau posters and prints by Michel Delacroix. "All of this is beautiful," explains the Frenchman, "but what really makes me feel good is when a customer says 'We were here three years ago, and nothing, absolutely nothing, has changed.'"

2120 Salzedo Street

LE SALADE MONTE CARLO

1 head Romaine lettuce
2 heads endive
1 tomato, cut into wedges
4 hearts of palm, halved
   lengthwise
6 mushrooms, sliced

FOR THE DRESSING:
2 teaspoons Dijon mustard
1 egg
2 tablespoons white
   wine vinegar
6 tablespoons vegetable oil
   Salt and pepper

1. Arrange the lettuces, hearts of palm, and mushrooms on chilled salad plates.

2. Prepare the dressing: Combine the mustard and egg in a large bowl. Add the vinegar, then gradually whisk in the oil. Season to taste with salt and pepper.

LE FILET DE RED SNAPPER DUGLERE
(Red Snapper with Tomato Cream Sauce)

2 red snappers
   (approximately
   4 pounds)
1 teaspoon chopped onions
2 cups peeled, seeded, and
   chopped tomatoes (see
   recipe page 4)

8 fresh medium-sized
   mushrooms, sliced
1 cup dry white wine
   Salt and pepper
2 cups heavy cream
1 tablespoon chopped
   parsley

1. Clean and trim the fish. Place the fish in a baking dish with onions, tomatoes, mushrooms, wine, salt, and pepper.

2. Cover the pan with parchment paper and place in a pre-heated 350° oven. Cook the fish for 20 minutes or until the fish flakes easily when pressed with a fork. Transfer the fish carefully to a serving platter.

3. Over high heat, boil the sauce until reduced by half. Add the cream and boil until reduced by half again. Pour the sauce over the fish and garnish with chopped parsley.

LE CARRE D'AGNEAU BOUQUETIERE
(Rack of Lamb)

2 racks of lamb, trimmed
   and oven ready
   Salt and fresh black pepper
2 tablespoons freshly
   chopped parsley

2 cloves garlic, chopped
2 tablespoons fresh
   bread crumbs

1. Preheat the oven to 375°. Season the lamb with salt and pepper.

2. Just before dinner, bake the lamb for 30 minutes (for medium rare), eight minutes more for medium. Combine the parsley, garlic, and bread crumbs. Spread this mixture over the lamb during the last 10 minutes of cooking.

SOUFFLÉ AU GRAND MARNIER WITH SABAYON SAUCE

1 cup milk
5 tablespoons sugar
4 tablespoons flour
5 eggs, separated

2 tablespoons Grand
   Marnier
SABAYON SAUCE

1. Preheat the oven to 375°. Thoroughly butter four 4–inch soufflé dishes and sprinkle the insides with sugar.

2. In a saucepan, bring ¾ cup of the milk to a boil with the sugar. In a bowl, mix the rest of the cold milk with the flour to make a smooth paste. Add the egg yolks and the Grand Marnier. Whisk in half of the heated milk and sugar, and return the mixture to the saucepan. Heat, stiring, almost to the boiling point and remove from heat. The mixture should be very smooth and thick.

3. Beat the egg whites to stiff peaks. Gently fold the whites into milk-yolk mixture. Spoon the soufflé mixture into the dishes, filling each ¾ full. Smooth the top. Bake the soufflés in the center of a preheated oven for 10 minutes. Serve immediately, with the *SABAYON SAUCE* on the side.

SABAYON SAUCE

2 egg yolks
3 tablespoons sugar
⅔ cup Cherry Herring

1 teaspoon almond extract
1 cup heavy cream

1. Beat the yolks in a stainless steel bowl with a wire whisk. Add the sugar and Cherry Herring.
2. Place the mixture over a pan of simmering water or in a double boiler, and cook, whisking constantly, just until the mixture thickens. Do not overcook. Remove the mixture from the heat, and continue whisking until the mixture cools to room temperature. Stir in the almond extract and set aside.
3. Whip the cream to stiff peaks. Fold it into the yolk mixture.

This sabayon sauce is delicious with a Grand Marnier Souffle, but it can also be served over fresh stawberries, raspberries, or other fruits.

Dinner For Six

Clams Casino

Onion Rings

Palm Lobster

Wine:

With the Lobster — Pouilly Fuissé

Bruce Bozi and Wally Ganzi, Owners

Tony Tammero, Chef

THE MIAMI PALM

Six months in Miami. Six months in East Hampton. That's not a bad way to spend your life. Just ask Tony Tammero, executive chef of the Palm. Tony's sister married Bruce Bozi, one of the owners of the Palm restaurant chain. For the past 21 years, he has gone from Palm to Palm, setting up the kitchens. Today, there are nine Palms in all, located in cities as far-flung as New York, Washington, Dallas, Los Angeles, and of course, Miami.

The Miami Palm may lack the sawdust on the floor of the original Palm in New York, but everything else is the same: the caricatures on the wall, the sturdy plank floors, the paddle fans whirling overhead. The restaurant seats 130, and the atmosphere is decidedly boisterous. "But we're not a hash house," says Tony with a smile. "After all, how many restaurants fly in lobster from Boston five times a week, and have prime beef delivered from New York in the company trucks?"

Lobster is definitely the house specialty. A typical Palm lobster weighs in at five pounds. Palm lobsters are grilled, not boiled as at most restaurants, and the chef bastes them with cream to protect the meat and to make them sweeter. They must be good: the Palm sells 1,500 pounds a week. Other highbrow specialities include Clams Casino, lamb chops and veal Milanese; but don't turn your nose up at the mounds of onion rings and homemade potato chips—the latter truly food for the gods!

The Palm is located in Seacoast Towers, next door to the Alexander Hotel, with its restaurant, Dominique's. Both hotels are owned by Stephen Muss, who, I would say, knows a thing or two about fine food.

5151 Collins Avenue
Miami Beach

CLAMS CASINO

3 dozen cherrystone clams
½ cup white wine
1 pound unsalted butter, at
   room temperature
4 tablespoons finely
   chopped shallots

1 bunch Italian (flat leaf)
   parsley, finely chopped
1 small green pepper,
   finely chopped
Salt and fresh black pepper
6 strips bacon, cut into
   1½ inch pieces

1. Scrub the clams thoroughly, discarding any with cracked shells. Place the clams in a large pot with the wine, and cook them, covered, over high heat, for 2 minutes, or until the shells just open. Let cool.

2. Meanwhile, cream the butter. Whisk in all flavorings, plus salt and pepper to taste.

3. Remove the top shell and arrange the clams in an ovenproof baking dish. Place a spoonful of flavored butter on each clam, and top with 2 pieces of bacon.

4. Just before serving, place the clams under the broiler and cook for 1 minute, or until the bacon is crisp and the butter, bubbling.

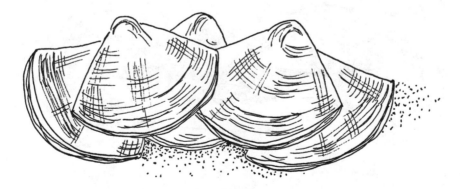

ONION RINGS

2 pounds large Bermuda onions	Salt and pepper
⅓ cup milk	3 cups oil, or more, for frying
1¼ cups flour	

1. Peel the onions and cut them into thin slices. Just before serving, dip the onions in milk, then in flour and seasonings, in a large bowl, and toss until blended.

2. Heat the oil to 375° and fry the onions for 8 minutes. Let them drain on paper towels for 6 minutes and serve at once.

The onion is hardly what one would call a gastronomic delicacy, and yet few dishes are more delectable than onion rings freshly fried. These have, alas, become an endangered species, along with French fries and homemade pies.

PALM LOBSTER

2 4 pound Maine lobsters   ½ cup clarified butter
¾ cup half and half

1. Cut the lobster in half, as described below. Remove the claws. Arrange the halves in a roasting pan. Pouring half and half over the lobsters.
2. Cook the lobsters under a preheated broiler for 8 minutes. Place the lobsters over the grill if you have one, or in a heavy frying pan, and cook over high heat for an additional 10 minutes.
3. Meanwhile, boil the claws for 10 minutes.
4. Just before serving, baste the lobsters with melted butter.

CLARIFIED BUTTER

To clarify butter, melt unsalted butter in a saucepan and skim off the foam that forms on top. Spoon the butter that remains into a measuring cup, leaving behind the milky water. When properly clarified, it will keep almost indefinitely.

This recipe is not for the faint-hearted, for the lobster must be cut while it is still alive. This is considerably more traumatic for the chef than for the lobster, for the latter is killed instantly. To split a live lobster, insert a large chopping knife through the head, directly behind the eyes. It is a good idea to hold the lobster with a pot holder to avoid cutting your hand on the spines. If you cannot bring yourself to cut the live lobster in half, place it in a pan with 1 inch of water, and boil it for 3 minutes to put it to sleep.

Dinner For Six

Mushrooms Stuffed with Crabmeat

Fresh Garden Salad Bowl

Roast Prime Rib of Beef

Creamed Spinach

Key Lime Pie

Flaming Spanish Coffee

Wines:

With the Mushrooms — Robert Mondavi Chardonnay, 1982

With the Beef — Alexander's Crown Cabernet Sauvignon, 1980

Marty Sussman and David Levy, Owners

Don't feel sorry for a guy like Marty Sussman. "Sometimes I kiss a hundred women a night, and my wife doesn't even get mad," he says. Sussman is the owner of Miami's popular New York Steak House, and kissing the ladies is all part of a night's work.

Marty and his partner David Levy remember most customers by their first names. This isn't as hard as it seems because their clientele reads like *Who's Who of Miami*. "This personal touch is part of what has made the New York Steak House so successful," says Sussman. "I want everyone to feel like a guest in my house."

You'd definitely call Sussman a meat and potatoes man. The New York Steak House serves only corn-fed, prime western beef. Steak sizes range from 12-18 ounces for a New York sirloin to 15-23 ounces for the house specialty, prime rib. Lobsters weigh in at three to six pounds, and are flown in daily from Boston.

There's nothing prissy about this steak joint. The blackboard menu offers the ominous warning, "We are not responsible for well done steaks." The walls of the restaurant are literally covered with photographs of the many celebrities who have dined here: Jackie Gleason, Henny Youngman, Alan King, Bob Hope, Milton Berle, Michael Jackson, Dan Marino, Jimmy Cefalo...the list goes on.

Last October, the New York Steak House moved to Biscayne Boulevard, and with Macy's up the block, it almost feels like New York.

17985 Biscayne Boulevard

MUSHROOMS STUFFED WITH CRABMEAT

30 large mushroom caps

FOR THE STUFFING:

1 pound fresh crabmeat,
  shells picked out
¾ cup bread crumbs
3 tablespoons finely
  chopped onions

3 tablespoons finely
  chopped celery
1 clove garlic, finely
  chopped
1 teaspoon finely chopped
  fresh parsley
2 eggs, beaten
¼ teaspoon salt
4 tablespoons butter

1. Quickly wash the mushrooms and remove the stems.
2. Combine the ingredients for the stuffing in a large bowl and mix thoroughly. Place a large spoonful of stuffing in each mushroom cap and arrange on a baking sheet. Top each mushroom cap with a piece of butter. Preheat oven to 350°.
3. Just before serving, bake the stuffed mushroom caps for 15 minutes or until golden brown. Serve at once.

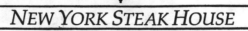

FRESH GARDEN SALAD BOWL

1½ heads of iceberg lettuce
1 red pepper, sliced
1 small red onion, sliced
½ cucumber, sliced
½ squash, sliced
¼ cup red cabbage, shredded
¼ cup bean sprouts

¼ cup radishes, sliced
4 rosettes of broccoli
4 rosettes of cauliflower
¼ cup shredded carrots
½ cherry tomatoes

ITALIAN DRESSING
(see below)

Combine all ingredients in a large bowl. Toss with *ITALIAN DRESSING*. Serve on chilled salad plates.

ITALIAN DRESSING

2 tablespoons diced red
  pepper
2 tablespoons diced onion
2 tablespoons diced carrot
2 tablespoons diced celery
1 cup sour cream

½ cups mayonnaise
1 clove garlic
1 tablespoon chopped
  parsley
1 tablespoon oregano
Salt and pepper to taste

Finely chop all vegetables in a food processor. Add the remaining ingredients and pureé until smooth. Chill for 24 hours before serving.

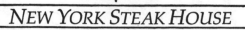

ROAST PRIME RIB OF BEEF

1   6 rib standing rib roast
      (about 12 pounds)
¼ cup salt
2   tablespoons pepper
2   tablespoons minced garlic

4   carrots, sliced
1   large onion, sliced
4   stalks celery, sliced
½ cup water
    JUS

1. Preheat oven to 325°.

2. Peel back the fat on the roast. Prepare a special seasoning by combining salt, pepper, and garlic, and rub this over the roast under the fat.

3. Place the vegetables and water in a roasting pan, and put the rib roast on top. Cook for approximately 1½ hours for medium rare. (The internal temperature for rare beef is 120°.) Reserve the pan juices. Meanwhile, prepare the beef stock below for the jus.

JUS

2   pounds beef bones
½ gallon water
1   onion, sliced

2   carrots, sliced
    Salt
    Pepper

1. Roast the bones in a preheated 400° oven for 1 hour. Add the vegetables and continue cooking until the vegetables are browned.

2. Place the bones and vegetables in a large pot, add water, and bring to a boil. Turn down the heat and continue cooking on a medium heat until reduced by half.

3. Strain the stock through a cheese cloth. Skim the fat off the reserved pan juices from the roast and add these juices to the stock. Serve JUS in a sauceboat on the side.

The secret to good prime rib is placing the seasoning under the fat. To obtain a tender prime rib, we cook it at a relatively low heat.

CREAMED SPINACH

1 pound frozen spinach, chopped
6 tablespoons butter
1 small onion, finely chopped
1 garlic clove, finely minced

½ cup flour
1 pint light cream
Salt
Fresh black pepper

1. Thaw the spinach. Heat the butter in a skillet and cook the onion and garlic for three minutes over medium heat until browned.

2. Stir in the flour and cook for 2 to 3 minutes over medium heat. Stir in the cream and simmer for 10 minutes, or until thickened.

3. Add the spinach and cook for 10 minutes on a low flame, stirring frequently. Season to taste with salt and pepper.

KEY LIME PIE

GRAHAM CRACKER CRUST
2 (14 ounce) cans sweetened condensed milk
2 eggs, beaten
6 ounces key lime juice

½ teaspoon grated key lime rind
1 cup heavy cream, stiffly whipped (for garnish)

1. Prepare the GRAHAM CRACKER CRUST. Preheat the oven to 325°.

2. In a large bowl combine all remaining ingredients except the whipped cream, and mix well. Pour this mixture into the crust and bake for 20 minutes, then chill for 24 hours. Garnish with whipped cream before serving.

GRAHAM CRACKER CRUST

2 cups graham cracker
   crumbs
½ cup brown sugar

1 tablespoon cinnamon
6 tablespoons melted butter

1. Combine all dry ingredients and mix well. Add the butter and mix until the dough is moist and pliable.

2. Press the dough into an 8-inch crust.

The key lime pie is indigenous to the Florida Keys, where a small yellow species of lime grows in the sub-tropical climate. Key lime juice is more sour than regular lime juice, so try to use the real thing.

FLAMING SPANISH COFFEE

1 cut lemon
   Approximately ½ cup
   sugar
6 ounces kahlua, plus some
   for sprinkling

6 ounces brandy
6 cups coffee
1 cup heavy cream, whipped
   until stiff

1. Rub the lemon around the rim of 6 glasses, then dip the glasses into the sugar. Hold each glass over a low flame until the sugar melts. Add 1 ounce each kahlua and brandy per glass and heat the glass by tipping it over an open flame to ignite the liquor. Flame for 1 minute. Add the coffee, top with fresh whipped cream, and a dash of kahlua.

THE PAVILLON GRILL

Dinner For Six

La Salade René

Petit Ragoût de Homard Printanièr

Tranche de Veau, Poëllée, Son Beurre au Citron

Terrine au Chocolat

Wines:

With the Lobster — Franciscan Chardonnay, 1979

With the Veal — Brouilly Chateau de la Chaize, 1981

Ted Gould, Owner

Guy Gateau, Màitre de Cuisine

THE PAVILLON GRILL

This is the house that Gould built. It soars 34 stories, with a panoramic view of Biscayne Bay. In the lobby stands a travertine marble sculpture by Henry Moore.

This is the restaurant that Gould built. The carpets are from Ireland; the green granite columns, from Brazil. The paintings of the world's great race courses are by the English artist, Peter Howell. The crystal is Venini; the silver is Calegaro from Italy; and the china is Royal Worchester.

And, Guy Gateau is the chef that Gould hired. Guy (whose last name appropriately means "cake" in French) was born in the French wine capital of Sancerre. Despite his youthful appearance, he is no newcomer to the restaurant business. Guy started at the age of 15, training with the legendary Alain Chapel in Mionnay. He also worked at a two-star restaurant on the Champs Elyées before opening his own restaurant, the Relais de Parc, in the town of Vichy.

Four years ago, the general manager of the Pavillon ate at Guy's restaurant. He called Gould that afternoon to rave about the Frenchman's cooking. Gould flew to France the next day, and the Pavillon had a chef. The Pavillon Grill opened February, 1983. Within six months, its contemporary cuisine and gracious French service gained the new restuarant wide critical acclaim.

"You can't create something from nothing," says Gateau. "You have to have tradition." To Guy, tradition means cooking without shortcuts, the way he always did in France. I asked him if there was anything else he would like the public to know about his restaurant. "Yes," replied the chef with a smile. "Our address."

Chopin Plaza

LA SALADE RENÉ
(Green Bean Salad with Chicken Livers and Truffles)

1 *pound* haricots verts *or very thin green beans*
Salt
1 *pound fresh green asparagus*
1 *pound fresh mushrooms, washed*
1 *ounce fresh or canned truffle*

FOR THE DRESSING:
4 *tablespoons butter*
6 *ounces chicken livers*
3 *tablespoons cognac*
2 *tablespoons mustard*
¼ *cup wine vinegar*
1 *scant cup hazelnut oil*
Salt and fresh black pepper
4 *tablespoons chopped fresh tarragon*
4 *tablespoons chopped fresh chervil*

1. Snap the green beans and cook them in 3 quarts rapidly boiling, heavily salted water for 3 minutes, or until crispy-tender. Immerse the beans in ice water to prevent overcooking.

2. Snap the fiberous ends off the asparagus; cook and refresh them, as described in step one.

3. Thinly slice the mushrooms. Thinly slice the truffles. If using canned truffles, be sure to reserve the juice for the dressing.

4. Prepare the dressing. Heat the butter in a small frying pan and sauté the chicken livers over high heat for 2 minutes—they should remain quite rare. Add the cognac and flambé. Purée the livers and press them through a sieve into a mixing bowl. Whisk in the mustard and vinegar. Gradually whisk in the hazelnut oil and salt and pepper to taste.

5. To assemble the salad: toss the vegetables with the dressing and arrange on salad plates. Sprinkle with the fresh herbs.

Haricots verts *are very thin species of green bean. If you can not find this luxury item in a specialty shop, use the smallest available beans.*

PETIT RAGOUT DE HOMARD PRINTANIER
(Spring Lobster Ragout)

½ pound pearl onions
½ pound baby carrots
½ pound new turnips
1 cup butter
2 teaspoons sugar
Salt
¼ pound snow peas
2 tomatoes, peeled, seeded, and chopped (see Page 4)
1½ pounds fresh fava beans

3½ pounds Maine lobsters
2 tablespoons flour
⅓ cup olive oil
6 garlic cloves, lightly crushed, with skins on
½ cups sherry
3 cups heavy cream
Juice of 2 lemons
Fresh black pepper
1 bunch chives, chopped

1. Clean and peel the onions, carrots, and turnips.

2. Cook the pearl onions with 2 tablespoons of the butter, the sugar, and a few tablespoons of water until they are tender and nicely glazed. Bring two pans of salted water to a boil. Add a tablespoon of butter to each and cook the baby carrots and new turnips separately just until they pierce easily with a fork. Drain and reserve the vegetables.

3. Remove the string from the sides of the snow peas and cook them in boiling water for 30 seconds or until they turn bright green. Drain and refresh with cold water.

4. In a small pan, cook the tomatoes for a few minutes to reduce the liquid and concentrate the flavor.

5. Shell the fava beans. Drop them into boiling water for 2 minutes. Cool in ice water and then remove the tough outer skin.

6. Kill the lobsters by dropping them into boiling water for 2 minutes. Separate the claws and the tails.

7. Remove the tamale from the heads. Melt ⅓ cup of the butter and mix it with the roe and the flour to make a light paste.

8. Heat the remaining butter with the olive oil and garlic in a skillet over medium heat. Add the lobster and cook it for 8 minutes. Add the sherry and cream and simmer for 3 minutes. Remove the lobster pieces and reserve.

9. Whisk the roe mixture into the sauce and simmer for 5 minutes, or until the sauce has reduced and thickened.

10. Place all the vegetables in a large saucepan. Strain the sauce over them. Shell the lobster meat and add it to the vegetables, cutting the tail section into several pieces. Keep the ragout warm, but do not let it boil. Serve in tureens or soup plates, sprinkled with chives.

This lobster stew may look complicated, but all the vegetables can be cooked ahead. In France, we would kill the lobsters by cutting them in half while alive. It may seem somewhat more humane to kill them in boiling water as described above. The tamale is the liver of the lobster—it looks like a greenish paste.

TRANCHE DE VEAU, POELLEESON BEURRE AU CITRON
(Medallions of Veal with Lemon Butter)

1½ pounds veal tenderloin or top round	Salt and pepper
8 lemons	¾ cup flour
½ cup sugar	¾ cup butter
1 cup water	½ cup dry white wine
2 tomatoes, peeled, seeded, and chopped (see page 4)	3 tablespoons chopped chives

1. Cut the veal into 18 steak-like medallions.

2. Using a vegetable peeler, remove 2 inch strips of the yellow zest from 4 lemons. Be careful not to take the bitter white pith. Cut the strips lengthwise into very fine slivers. Blanch these slivers in two separate batches of boiling water, then drain. In a small saucepan, heat the sugar with the water, stirring, and simmer until the syrup is clear. Add the lemon zest and simmer for 5 minutes. Let the zest cool in the syrup.

3. Using a sharp paring knife, cut the white pith away from the 4 lemons, then cut each lemon segment away from the membrane, and reserve. Squeeze the juice from the remaining lemons and reserve.

4. Cook the chopped tomatoes for a few minutes in a saucepan over medium heat to evaporate some of the liquid.

5. Season the veal medallions with salt and pepper, and lightly dust with flour. In a large frying pan, melt half the butter. Sauté the medallions, in several batches (so that they do not touch), for 1 minute per side or until lightly browned. Remove the medallions from the pan and keep warm.

6. Pour off all the fat from the pan and deglaze it with white wine. Simmer until only ⅓ cup wine remains. Stir in the lemon juice and strain the sauce into a small saucepan. Add the lemon segments. Cut the remaining butter into small pieces, and stir them into the sauce, one by one. Keep the sauce warm.

7. Arrange two veal medallions on each plate. Remove the lemon zest from the syrup with a fork, and arrange some slivers on top of each medallion. Sprinkle the veal with tomato and season it well with freshly ground pepper. (The veal may be kept warm in a 200° oven for a few minutes). Just before serving, spoon some sauce on the side of the medallions, and sprinkle with chopped chives.

A medallion of veal is a small, thick steak. The zest of a lemon is the oil-rich outer rind. To deglaze a pan, one adds an acidic liquid, like wine, to dissolve congealed meat juices.

TERRINE AU CHOCOLAT
(Chocolate Terrine)

8 ounces unsweetened chocolate, cut into small pieces

8 ounces sweet chocolate, cut into small pieces

½ pound fondant

3-4 tablespoons cognac or bourbon

3 tablespoons instant coffee

½ cup butter, softened

1 cup heavy cream, whipped to soft peaks

1. Melt the chocolate in a double boiler. Melt the fondant in the same way and combine it with the chocolate.

2. Heat the cognac or bourbon. Dissolve the instant coffee in it and stir it into the chocolate. Cool the chocolate mixture to room temperture.

3. Combine the cooled chocolate mixture with the softened butter and mix well. Fold in the cream. Spoon the mixture into a 4-cup terrine mold or loaf pan and refrigerate overnight.

4. Before serving, dip the mold quickly in lukewarm water. Unmold the terrine on a platter. Serve with additional whipped cream, if desired, and cookies. Serves 10.

Traditionally, a terrine is a sort of meat loaf made with pork and served cold with mustard. This one is made with chocolate and served as a dessert. Fondant is a special icing—it is available at any bakery supply store.

RAIMONDO'S

Dinner For Four

Artichokes Dolomiti

Cannelloni Excelsior

Veal Chops Tre Corone

Cheesecake Raimondo

Wines:

With the Artichokes — Verdicchio di Montanello, 1983

With the Veal — Chianti Classico, 1979

Jule Laudisio, Owner

Carmelo Miranda, Executive Chef

"**B**ehind every successful man is a woman," the saying goes. So successful is Jule that Raimondo is not at Raimondo's anymore. Raimondo's is an Italian restaurant in Coral Gables, formerly run by Jule and Raimando Laudisio. Although Jule and Raimondo have gone their separate ways, Jule has proven that the show must go on.

You will find here the same classic Italian menu as before. You will also find the same red carnations and white table cloths, the same Tiffany-style lamps and cedar walls. Curiously, what you won't find here are any Italian waiters. "As a woman, I found it easier to deal with Latins," says Jule, and as a result, the whole staff is Latin.

The staff may be Latin, but the food is authentically Italian. Veal chops are the house specialty. These are enormous chops, like the rack of veal "Chef Bocuse," named for Paul Bocuse, the French founder of *nouvelle cuisine*, or the veal chop "Pavarotti," stuffed with pâté and topped with Bordelaise sauce. Be sure, however, to save room for dessert, for the almond meringue "Atlas" is a real show stopper.

A woman's touch is evident in the silk flower arrangement and paintings by local artists. And according to Jule Laudisio, there's a lot more decorating to come.

4612 S.W. Le Jeune Road

ARTICHOKES DOLOMITI

4 large artichokes	1 cup heavy cream
Salt	2 egg yolks
Juice of 1 lemon	12 ounces lump crabmeat
8 tablespoons melted butter	4 mushrooms, thinly sliced
Pepper	Fresh grated nutmeg
4 tablespoons chopped shallots	4 ounces freshly grated Parmesan cheese
2 anchovy fillets	4 tablespoons bread crumbs
1 tablespoon chopped capers	Paprika
4 tablespoons dry vermouth	

1. Trim the points off the artichoke leaves and cut off the stems. Cook the artichokes in rapidly boiling, salted water until tender, but still a little firm. Let cool

2. Remove the outside leaves and scrape out the "choke" with a grapefruit spoon.

3. Place the artichokes in an ovenproof baking dish and sprinkle with lemon juice, 4 tablespoons melted butter, salt, and freshly ground black pepper.

4. Meanwhile, prepare the stuffing. Sauté the shallots in 4 tablespoons melted butter over medium heat until soft. Add the anchovies, capers, and vermouth and simmer for 1 minute. Add the cream and boil the mixture until three-quarters of the original volume remains.

5. Remove the pan from the heat and beat in the egg yolks. Fold in the crab meat, mushrooms, and nutmeg, salt, and pepper to taste.

6. Spoon the stuffing into the center of the artichokes. Dot the tops with Parmesan cheese, bread crumbs, and paprika. Bake the stuffed artichokes in a preheated 350° oven for 10 minutes or until golden brown.

CANNELLONI EXCELSIOR

CREPES (see below)

3 tablespoons butter
6 ounces sweet sausage meat
6 ounces coarse-ground veal
4 ounces coarse-ground beef
1 medium onion, chopped
1 clove garlic, minced
Freshly grated nutmeg

Salt and freshly ground black pepper
4 tablespoons red wine
2 ounces prosciutto, finely chopped
4 ounces freshly grated Parmesan cheese
6 ounces ricotta cheese
6 ounces chopped cooked spinach
CREAM SAUCE

1. Prepare the CREPES.

2. Meanwhile, prepare the filling. Melt the butter in a large frying pan. Sauté the sausage, veal, and beef over medium heat for 5 minutes, or until lightly browned. Add the onion, garlic, and seasonings. Cook for five minutes or until the onion is transparent. Pour off the excess fat, add the wine, and cook until reduced by half.

3. Remove the pan from the heat and mix in the prosciutto, cheeses, and spinach. Add the egg yolks and mix thoroughly.

4. Place a heaping spoonful of filling in the center of each crêpe and roll the crêpe up like a cigar. Arrange the crêpes in a buttered baking dish and pour the CREAM SAUCE on top. Bake the CANNELLONI EX-CELSIOR in a preheated 350° oven for 20 minutes or until lightly browned.

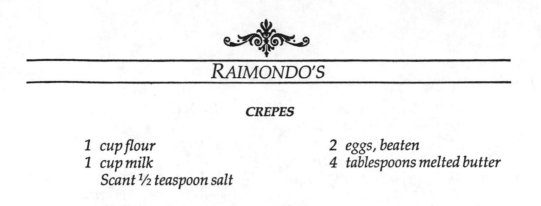
CREPES

1 cup flour	2 eggs, beaten
1 cup milk	4 tablespoons melted butter
Scant ½ teaspoon salt	

1. Combine all the ingredients in a blender.
2. Heat 6 inch crêpe pans over a medium heat. Off the heat, all at once, add 3 tablespoons batter. Cook the crêpe for 30 seconds per side. Turn it with a spatula and cook for 20 seconds. Continue making crêpes until all batter is used up.

CREAM SAUCE

1 cup heavy cream	1 egg yolk
1 bay leaf	Salt and pepper
2 cloves garlic, peeled	Freshly grated nutmeg

1. Simmer the cream, bay leaf, and garlic in a heavy saucepan until reduced by ¼.
2. Place the yolk in a heat-proof bowl. Strain the cream in a very thin stream into the yolk, whisking vigorously. Add salt, pepper, and freshly grated nutmeg to taste.

VEAL CHOPS TRE CORONE

4 thick veal chops
Salt and fresh black pepper
4 tablespoons extra virgin
olive oil
4 shallots, chopped
1 sprig fresh rosemary
1 sprig fresh sage
¾ cup Chianti wine

2 teaspoons unsalted butter
Juice of one lemon
4 ounces prosciutto, diced
6 ounces fontina cheese,
grated
4 ounces Bel Paese, grated
¼ cup heavy cream

1. Season the chops with salt and pepper. Heat the oil in a large skillet over high heat and brown the chops on both sides. Place the veal chops in an oven proof baking dish.

2. To the pan juices add half the shallots, the rosemary, sage, and Chianti. Boil the mixture until reduced by half. Add 1 teaspoon butter and the lemon juice; simmer for 1 minute. Pour this sauce over the chops.

3. Prepare the topping. In another skillet, melt the remaining 1 teaspoon butter and sauté the remaining shallots and prosciutto for 1 minute. Remove the pan from the heat, and stir in the cheeses and cream. Spoon this topping onto the veal.

4. Bake the veal in a preheated 400° oven for 20 minutes, or until the chops are cooked and the cheese is bubbling and browned.

This dish is a rich blend of veal, prosciutto, and Italian cheeses. Fontina is a creamy cheese with a pungent flavor. Bel Paese has a pleasantly bitter flavor. For the best results, use imported Italian cheese.

CHEESECAKE RAIMONDO

1½ *pounds cream cheese*
1½ *pounds butter*
½ *pound sugar*
4 *eggs*
2 *egg yolks*

½ *cup sour cream*
½ *teaspoon vanilla*
¼ *cup amaretto*
Grated rind from 1 lemon

1. Cream the cream cheese and butter with the sugar. Beat the eggs and yolks in one by one. Beat in the remaining ingredients.

2. Thickly butter a 10 inch springform pan and sprinkle the inside with flour. Bring 1 inch of water to a boil in a roasting pan. Spoon the cheesecake mixture into the pan and place it in the roasting pan. Bake the cheesecake in a preheated 350° oven for 40-50 minutes, or until just set. Turn off the oven and wait 1 hour before removing the cheesecake. Chill thoroughly before serving.

This cheesecake is so good, it doesn't even need a crust. We bake it in a bain marie, *that is, a pan of simmering water, which prevents it from drying out. Leaving the cheesecake in the oven for 1 hour after baking helps prevent the center from falling. Serves 8-12.*

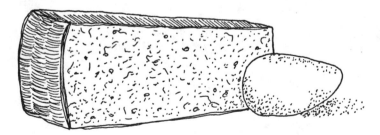

REGINE'S

Dinner For Six

Salade Tropicale

Les Oeufs Brouillés aux Caviar

Noisettes d'Agneau àl'Ail Confit

Marquise de Chocolat

Wines:

With the Eggs—Corton Charlemagne, Bonneau du Martray, 1980

With the Lamb—Cos d'Estournel, 1976

Regine, Owner

Daniel Theme, Executive Chef

L et the Guide Michelin have its three-star restaurants in France. I have found my own three-star right here in Miami: Regine's. This chic restaurant reigns very privately from the top floor of the magnificent Grand Bay Hotel in Coconut Grove.

The food arrives on the oversized plates that have become the calling card of French nouvelle cuisine. The man responsible for the dinner is Daniel Theme, a chef born in Nîmes, a city in France that gave its name to a popular fabric: denim. "As a child, I dreamed of Regine—her music that is," say the chef, "but I never dreamed that someday I would work for her." Daniel comes by his calling naturally: his father owned a one-star restaurant in Soup-sur-Loing; his brother owns a one-star restaurant in the scenic town of Les Baux.

The biggest star, however, is Regine herself, a French chanteuse who has been likened to the immortal Piaf. Her real genius lay in opening nightclubs for the rich and famous. To date, there are 15 Regine's around the world, with only two in the U.S. The Miami branch opened in December, 1983.

Regine's has everything you would expect of a private club: mirrored ceilings, a red and black color scheme, and seats for an intimate 80. The food is presented with a visual artistry worthy of the decor. Patrons feast on such innovative dishes as *les ouefs poule au caviar* (scrambled eggs and caviar), *noisettes d'agneau à l' ail confit* (lamb medallions with candied garlic), and *marquise au chocolat* (mousse cake) for dessert.

Technically, Regine's is a private club, but hotel guests are also welcomed. Don't despair: if you're not lucky enough to be a member, you can always book a room at the Grand Bay!

2669 South Bay Shore Drive
Coconut Grove

SALADE TROPICALE

3 tomatoes, peeled and
    seeded (see instructions
    on page 4)
A handful of fresh basil
    leaves, chopped
Salt and fresh black pepper
3 heads radicchio
2 heads Belgian endive
3 heads bibb lettuce
6 cooked artichoke hearts
3 cooked lobster tails,
    shelled and cut into
    ½ inch pieces

6 (1-ounce) slices smoked
    salmon, cut into ½-inch
    pieces
6 slices fresh pineapple, core
    removed, cut into
    wedges
6 large mushrooms, thinly
    sliced
TROPICAL SALAD
    DRESSING (see below)

1. Cut the tomato into ¼ inch cubes, and combine with the basil leaves, salt and pepper. Wash and dry the lettuce leaves. Cut the lobster and salmon. Slice the pineapple and mushrooms. Prepare the dressing.

2. Arrange the lettuces on the plates, leaving the middle open. Place an artichoke in the center of each plate and fill it with tomato mixture. Arrange the lobster slices around the artichokes. Sprinkle the smoked salmon pieces on top of the lettuce. Arrange the pineapple wedges and sliced mushrooms on top. The salad should look colorful and artistic, but the ingredients should not be stiffly symmetrical.

3. Spoon the *TROPICAL SALAD DRESSING* on top and serve at once.

This colorful salad is typical of nouvelle cuisine *in its unusual combination of flavors. Radicchio is a variety of lettuce that resembles a tiny red cabbage. Its gently bitter flavor is very much in vogue. Instructions on cooking and hollowing out artichokes are found on page 121.*

SALADE TROPICALE DRESSING

2 tablespoons Dijon-style
   mustard
Salt and fresh black pepper
Juice of 2 fresh limes
3 tablespoons vinegar
2 tablespoons very finely
   chopped shallots

¾ cup olive oil
1 small bunch fresh
   marjoram,
   finely chopped
1 ounces parboiled ginger,
   grated

Combine the first five ingredients in a heavy bowl. Gradually whisk in the oil, followed by the marjoram and fresh ginger. Add additional salt or pepper as necessary. Let the dressing stand at least 30 minutes before serving.

LES OEUFS BROUILLES AUX CAVIAR
(Scrambled Eggs with Caviar)

6 large eggs
Salt and fresh black pepper
½ cup heavy cream
   bunch fresh dill, finely
   chopped

1 bunch fresh chives,
   finely chopped
FISH SAUCE
2 ounces beluga caviar

1. Thoroughly beat the eggs with the salt, pepper, cream, and half the fresh chopped herbs.

2. Melt the butter in a stainless steel frying pan, and cook the eggs over a low heat, stirring with a spatula: the eggs should be very loose. Spoon the eggs into the center of 6 warm dinner plates.

3. Spoon the herbed FISH SAUCE on one side of the eggs, and the regular FISH SAUCE on the other. place a generous spoonful of caviar on top.

To an American, scrambled eggs are something you have for breakfast. The French cook them as delicate and smooth as hollandaise sauce, to be served as the most luxurious of appetizers. Beluga is the largest grade of sturgeon caviar. The effect will be totally ruined if you use inexpensive caviar, like lumpfish.

FISH SAUCE

1 cup fish stock (see recipe
   on page 167)
1 cup heavy cream
2 tablespoons tomato paste

Salt and fresh black pepper
Chopped dill and chives
   from above

1. Combine the first three ingredients in a heavy saucepan and gently simmer for 15 minutes, or until the sauce is slightly thickened. Correct the seasoning with salt and pepper.

2. Pour half the sauce into another pan and stir in the fresh herbs, creating *HERBED FISH SAUCE.*

NOISETTES D' AGNEAU A L'AIL CONFIT
(Lamb Medallions with Candied Garlic)

3 small racks of lamb
   Salt and fresh black pepper
3 tablespoons olive oil
3 ripe tomatoes, peeled
   and seeded
2 sprigs fresh rosemary,
   chopped, plus 2 sprigs
   for garnish

1 sprig fresh basil, chopped
⅓ cup cognac
1 cup demi-glace (see recipe
   on page 55)
1 cup heavy cream
   CANDIED GARLIC

1. Season the lamb with salt and pepper. Roast the racks in a preheated 400° oven for 20 minutes (for medium rare) or until cooked to taste.

2. Meanwhile, prepare the sauce. Heat the olive oil in a skillet. Add the tomatoes, rosemary, basil, and garlic, and cook for 3 minutes over high heat. Add the cognac and flambé. Reduce the heat, add the demi-glace and cream, and simmer the sauce for 10 minutes. Keep warm.

3. When lamb is cooked to taste, transfer it to a cutting board, and let stand for 3 minutes. Carve the meat off the ribs. (To do this, simply run the knife along the inside of the ribs.) Cut each loin into ½ inch slices. Spoon the sauce onto a warm platter and arrange the lamb on top. Garnish with sprigs of fresh rosemary and *CANDIED GARLIC*.

Provence, where this recipe originated, is a region in the south of France, famed for its garlic, tomatoes, and fresh herbs (not to mention its glamorous Mediterranean seacoast). Have your butcher trim the fat off the racks of lamb—it is not necessary to French the ribs, as the meat will be carved from the bone for serving.

AIL CONFIT
Candied Garlic

3 heads garlic, broken into
   cloves and peeled
1 cup milk
3 tablespoons butter

2 tablespoons sugar
1 tablespoon water
   Salt and white pepper

1. Break the garlic into cloves and peel each one as described above. Combine the garlic and milk in a saucepan and gently simmer for 5-10 minutes, or until soft. Drain the garlic and blot it dry.

2. Combine the remaining ingredients in a saucepan and boil for 1 minute. Add the garlic cloves and cook over high heat for 1 minute, or until the cloves are coated with a shiny, syrupy glaze.

Garlic looses its pungency when cooked, and it makes an unusual vegetable. To peel garlic, lightly crush it with the side of a knife to split the skin. Slip off the skins with your fingers.

MARQUISE AU CHOCOLAT

FOR THE SPONGE CAKE:

- 6 eggs
- ⅔ cup sugar
- 1 tablespoon vanilla
  Pinch of salt and cream of tartar
- 1¼ cups flour
- 6 tablespoons unsalted butter, at room temperature, plus 2 tablespoons melted butter for buttering the pan

FOR THE CHOCOLATE FILLING:

- ½ pound semi-sweet chocolate
- ½ cup water
- 1 stick unsalted butter, at room temperature
- 3 cups heavy cream
- ½ cup Grand Marnier
- 1 tablespoon instant coffee dissolved in 1 tablespoon boiling water
- 1 tablespoon Kahlua
  COFFEE SAUCE

1. Prepare the sponge cake. Separate the eggs. Beat the yolks with all but 3 tablespoons sugar with a mixer or by hand for 5 minutes. Whisk in the vanilla. Set aside. Brush a jelly roll pan with melted butter, chill, and brush it again with butter.

2. Beat the egg whites with a pinch of salt and cream of tartar. When the egg whites reach soft peaks, add the sugar and continue beating the whites to stiff peaks.

3. Gently fold the whites into the yolk mixture, sifting in the flour. Gently fold in the butter. Spread the mixture in the buttered pan.

4. Bake the sponge cake in a preheated 250° oven for 20 minutes or until firm. Remove the pan from the oven and invert the cake onto a rack.

5. Prepare the filling. Melt the chocolate in the water. Whisk in the butter, 1 cup cream, and the Grand Marnier. Beat the remaining cream to stiff peaks, and fold it into the chocolate mixture with the coffee and Kahlua.

6. Line a long, narrow loaf pan or terrine mold with waxed paper. Cut the sponge cake into strips the size of the sides and bottom of the mold, and use these to line the sides and bottom. Spoon the chocolate mixture into the mold. Cut a strip from the remaining sponge cake and arrange it on top. Chill the marquise in the freezer for at least 3 hours.

7. To serve, dip the mold in warm water for 10 seconds, and invert the marquise onto a cutting board. Dip a long, slender knife in boiling water, and use it to cut the marquise into ½ inch slices. Spoon the *COFFEE SAUCE* onto chilled dessert plates and place a slice of marquise in the center.

COFFEE SAUCE

3 egg yolks
½ cup sugar
2 tablespoons flour
2 tablespoons instant coffee
dissolved in boiling
water

½ cup Kahlua
2 tablespoons vanilla
2 cups heavy cream

1. Whisk the egg yolks with the sugar in a heat-proof bowl. Whisk in the flour and flavorings.

2. Meanwhile, bring the cream to a boil in a heavy saucepan. Gradually whisk the cream into the yolk mixture. Return the mixture to the pan, and simmer it for 2 minutes over low heat whisking vigorously. (You must whisk vigorously, or the sauce will burn.) Transfer the sauce back to the bowl and cool.

"The Spoonbill"

Dinner For Four

Ratatouille De Saumon Aux Poivrons Rouges

Tian D' Agneau Au Porto

Parfait Au Fraises

Wines:

With the Salmon — Grgich Hills Chardonnay, 1981

*With the Lamb — Chateau Montelena
Cabernet Sauvignon, 1976*

Eduardo Arellano, Owner

"**If** music be the food of love, play on," mused Shakespeare's Duke Orsino. You'll find here not only live music (on weekends), but dancing, fine dining, and hovering service. Etched glass, mirrored columns, floral fabric chairs, and colorful murals are but a few of the attractions that make the Spoonbill such a magnificent place to dine.

The man responsible for this Key Biscayne dining spot is Eduardo R. Arellano. The man responsible for the lavish decor is Mario R. Arellano, Eduardo's father! The menu covers were drawn by Miami artist, Arthur Singer. Although the spoonbill is on the endangered species list, it lives on in the breathtaking murals.

The food at the Spoonbill is boldly contemporary, featuring such innovations as salmon "ratatouille," mallard duck in three pepper sauce, and a "mirror" of chocolate and lime. The fresh *foie gras*, served in a raspberry sauce, comes from New York State, but it is made by the old-fashioned method. It is one of the best dishes I have ever tasted— either in Miami, or France.

Naturally, there's an à la carte menu, but the Spoonbill offers two fixed menus for people who can't decide. The *fraicheur de Floride* menu features native Floridian specialities, while the *menu prestige* comes with no fewer than six individual courses.

Like the Spoonbill, which returns again and again to its nest, you will find yourself returning again and again to this lovely restaurant in the Key Biscayne Hotel and Villa.

701 Ocean Drive

RATATOUILLE DE SAUMON AUX POIVRONS ROUGES
(Salmon "Ratatouille")

1 *large red bell pepper,*
   cored and seeded
1 *8 inch zucchini*
1 *medium-sized onion*
2 *tablespoons olive oil*
½ *teaspoon fresh thyme*
   Salt and fresh black pepper
2 *tablespoons olive oil*
1 *small eggplant, peeled*
1 *tomato, peeled, seeded,*
   and chopped (see recipe
   on page 4)

2 *tablespoons finely*
   chopped shallots
2 *teaspoons minced fresh*
   garlic
1 *tablespoon chopped fresh*
   basil
   Salt and pepper
1 *pound fresh salmon fillets*
   Softened butter, for
   buttering the molds
4 *small oven-proof bowls or*
   ramekins

1. Prepare the pepper mixture. Cut the pepper, zucchini, and onions into thin slivers. Heat the olive oil in a small frying pan and sauté the vegetables with thyme, salt, and pepper over a medium heat for 3-4 minutes, or until tender. Set aside.

2. Prepare the eggplant mixture. Heat the olive oil in a small frying pan and sauté the eggplant, tomato, and flavorings over medium heat for 3-4 minutes, or until tender. Add salt and pepper to taste. Set aside.

3. Prepare the salmon. Run your fingers over the top of the fillet to locate any bones. Pull out the bones with a tweezers. Cut the salmon into thin, diagonal slices. Brush the bowls or ramekins with the butter. Use the salmon slices to line the molds, saving 4 small pieces for the tops.

4. Assemble the individual ratatouilles. Divide the pepper mixture between the four molds. Spoon the eggplant mixture on top. Place the

remaining salmon over the eggplant. Set the bowls in a roasting pan in ½ inch boiling water. Bake in a preheated 300° oven for 8-10 minutes, or until the salmon is opaque. To serve, invert the bowls onto warm dinner plates to unmold the individual ratatouilles.

Ratatouille is a cold vegetable salad from the south of France made with eggplant and green peppers. The twist here comes with adding the poached salmon. A domed effect is achieved by baking the ratatouille in small bowls.

TIAN D'AGNEAU AU PORTO
(Lamb with Spinach and Port)

1 (1 pound) boned loin of lamb	¾ pound mushrooms, washed and thinly sliced
Salt and fresh black pepper	1 tomato, peeled, seeded and diced (see recipe on page 4)
4 tablespoons unsalted butter	
½ pound fresh spinach, stemmed and washed	4 fresh basil leaves
	PORT SAUCE

1. Sprinkle the lamb with salt and pepper. Place it in a preheated 400° oven and roast it for 15 minutes, or until cooked to taste.

2. Meanwhile, melt 2 tablespoons butter in a skillet and sauté the spinach over high heat for 1 minute, or until tender. Season with salt and pepper. Melt the remaining butter in another skillet, and sauté the mushrooms over high heat for 1 minute, or until tender. Season to taste. Combine the spinach and mushrooms.

3. Carve the lamb into ⅛ inch thick slices. Mound the spinach mixture in the center of each of four hot dinner plates. Arrange the lamb slices around the spinach. Spoon the *PORT SAUCE* on top. Garnish each dish with diced tomato and place a fresh basil leaf in the center.

PORT SAUCE

2 cups demi-glace (see recipe on page 55)	4 tablespoons unsalted butter
¼ cup port wine	Salt and fresh black pepper
2 tablespoons dry white wine	

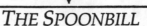

1. Combine the first 3 ingredients, and simmer for 5 minutes.
2. Remove the sauce from the heat and whisk in the butter, little by little. Season the sauce with salt and fresh black pepper.

STRAWBERRY PARFAIT

3 egg whites
Pinch each of salt and
   cream of tartar
1 scant cup sugar
¼ cup water

1 pint strawberries
¼ cup confectioner's sugar
   (or to taste)
1 cup heavy cream, beaten
   to stiff peaks

1. Prepare an Italian meringue. Beat the egg whites to stiff peaks in a mixer, adding the salt and cream of tartar after 20 seconds. As the whites stiffen, sprinkle in 2 tablespoons sugar.

2. Meanwhile, combine the remaining sugar and water in a saucepan and cook over high heat until the mixture reaches 239° on a sugar thermometer. Pour the boiling sugar syrup over the whites in a thin stream and continue beating until the mixture is cool.

3. Wash and hull the strawberries. Reserve six pretty berries for garnish. Purée the remaining berries in a blender or food processor with sugar to taste. Beat the cream to stiff peaks.

4. To assemble the parfaits, fold the strawberry purée and whipped cream into the meringue. Spoon this mixture into four champagne flutes. Freeze for at least 4 hours or overnight. Just before serving, garnish each parfait with a fresh strawberry.

This parfait owes its creaminess to Italian meringue, a preparation made by mixing boiling sugar syrup into stiffly beaten egg whites. The trick is to beat the egg whites slowly and pour the syrup over them as soon as they are stiff.

TIBERIO

Dinner For Six

Asparagi All' Agro

Mozzarella Bella

Linguine All' Aragosta

Profiteroles

Wines:

With the Lobster—Cortese Di Gabi, 1982

With the Cream Puffs—Asti Spumante

Julio Santillo, Owner

S aks Fifth Avenue to your left. Neiman Marcus to your right. I would say that Tiberio keeps very good company in the fashionable Bal Harbor Mall.

Tiberio is the twin of a like-named restaurant in Washington, D.C. Both restaurants are owned by a Neopolitan businessman named Julio Santillo. Santillo left out the usual hanging grapes, Chianti bottles, and Italian travel posters, when he opened Tiberio seven years ago. Instead, he draped the tables with elegant pink cloths and filled the room with roses. The flowers are imported from Columbia; the restaurant goes through 1000 pink roses for the tables and 800 red roses for the ladies each week.

The first thing you see on entering Tiberio is a magnificent dessert table. But you can't have the *profiteroles* (cream puffs with chocolate sauce), *zuppa inglese* (booze and custard-soaked cake) or other desserts, until you have finished your dinner. This is not very difficult, considering the fine job the kitchen does with such Italian classics as *linguini all' aragosta* (pasta with lobster), *vitello "Tiberio"* (veal with mushrooms, truffles, and ham), and *melanzane al funghetto* (eggplant with mushrooms).

The restaurant seats 220, amid white stucco arches and cylindrical, hanging black lamps. After-dinner drinks are complimentary, as are the Godiva chocolates. And, ladies, don't leave without your complimentary red rose.

9700 Collins Avenue
Bal Harbour

ASPARAGI ALL'AGRO

1½ pounds fresh asparagus
    Salt
  1 teaspoon Dijon mustard
    Salt and fresh black pepper
  ¼ teaspoon minced fresh
    garlic

½ teaspoon dried oregano
4 tablespoons fresh lemon
   juice
1 cup olive oil

1. Snap the asparagus. Bring at least 2 quarts water to a rolling boil with 2 teaspoons salt. Boil the asparagus for 2 minutes, or until just tender. Refresh under cold running water and drain.

2. Prepare the dressing. Combine the mustard, salt, pepper, garlic, oregano, and lemon juice and whisk until smooth. Gradually whisk in the oil. Correct the seasoning.

3. To serve, arrange the asparagus on chilled salad plates. Spoon the dressing on top.

To snap asparagus, hold the botton in one hand and bend the top with the other hand. The asparagus will snap at the natural break.

MOZZARELLA BELLA

2 pounds fresh mozzarella
   cheese
1 cup milk
1 cup flour
2 eggs, beaten
1 cup fresh bread crumbs

2 cups oil, for frying
12 anchovy fillets
½ teaspoon minced garlic
⅓ cup olive oil
   Lemon wedges, for
    serving

1. Cut the mozzarella into ½ inch slices. Cut each slice into 2 triangles. Dip each triangle first in milk, then in flour, then in egg, finally in bread crumbs.

2. Heat the oil to 350° in a frying pan. Fry the triangles in the oil for 1 minute, or until golden brown. Arrange the fried cheese in a shallow baking dish and top with anchovy fillets, garlic, and the olive oil.

3. Bake the cheese in a preheated 450° oven for 5 minutes. Serve at once.

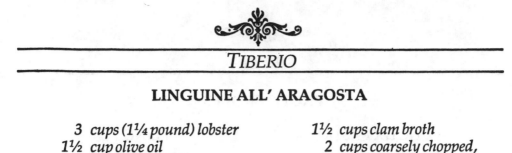

LINGUINE ALL' ARAGOSTA

3 cups (1¼ pound) lobster	1½ cups clam broth
1½ cup olive oil	2 cups coarsely chopped,
1 teaspoon minced fresh	peeled, seeded tomatoes
garlic	(see instructions on
½ teaspoon hot Italian	page 4)
pepper	Salt, to taste
	2 pounds fresh linguine

1. Cut the lobsters in half. Heat ½ cup olive oil in a large frying pan and fry the lobsters, cut side down, for 2 minutes, or until the meat is white. (See instructions on page 101)

2. Meanwhile, prepare the sauce. Combine the garlic, pepper, clam juice and tomatoes in a large saucepan and simmer for 5 minutes. Correct the seasoning. Add the sauce to the lobster and gently simmer for 5 minutes, or until the lobster is cooked.

3. Just before serving, cook the linguini in at least 4 quarts rapidly boiling, lightly salted water. When cooked *al dente* (still a little chewy), drain the pasta and divide it between 6 large plates. Place a half lobster on each mound of pasta and spoon the sauce on top.

This dish is a version of that Italian classic, lobster fra diavolo. *The chef cuts the lobster in half while it is still alive. If you don't have the courage to do this, boil the lobster for 3 minutes first.*

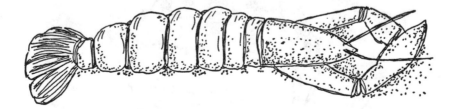

PROFITEROLES

CHOUX PASTRY:

- 1 stick unsalted butter
- 1 cup water
- ½ teaspoon salt
- 1 teaspoon sugar
- 1 cup flour
- 5 eggs

FILLING:

- 3 egg yolks
- 4 tablespoons sugar
- ½ teaspoon vanilla
- 3 tablespoons flour
- 1 cup milk
- Butter, for dotting the top
- CHOCOLATE SAUCE

1. Prepare the choux pastry. Combine the butter, water, and salt in a heavy saucepan. Bring the mixture to a boil. Sift in the flour and cook the mixture for 1 minute, stirring with a wooden spoon. Remove the pan from the heat, and beat in the eggs one by one.

2. Spoon the dough into a piping bag fitted with a ½ inch round top. Pipe the dough into ¾ inch balls on a baking sheet, leaving 2 inches between each mound. Bake the profiteroles in a preheated 400° oven for 45 minutes, or until the balls are puffed and golden brown. Make a tiny slit in the side of each profiterole to release the steam and cool on a cake rack.

3. Prepare the filling. Beat the egg yolks, sugar, and vanilla in a mixer for 5 minutes. Add the flour and beat just to mix. Meanwhile, bring

the milk to a boil and add it, little by little, to the yolk mixture. Return the mixture to the saucepan and simmer it gently for 5 minutes, whisking constantly. Remove the pan from the heat, dot the filling with butter and let it cool. Prepare the *CHOCOLATE SAUCE.*

4. To assemble the profiteroles, spoon the filling into a pastry bag fitted with a ¼ inch round tip. Squirt 1 tablespoon filling into each pastry shell. To serve, place three profiteroles on a dessert plate and spoon the *CHOCOLATE SAUCE* on top.

CHOCOLATE SAUCE

½ *pound Hershey's fudge syrup*
½ *pound cocoa powder*
1¼ *pounds semi-sweet chocolate*

1 *cup heavy cream*
¼ *cup confectioners sugar, or to taste*

Combine the ingredients in a saucepan and gently simmer over a low heat until the sauce is smooth. Add sugar to taste.

Profiteroles are cream puffs with custard and topped with hot chocolate sauce. This recipe will serve 6-8.

Veronique's

Dinner For Four

Radicchio and Bibb Lettuce Salad with Tarragon Dressing

Lobster Bisque

Chicken Armagnac

Pears Burgundy

Wines:

With the Bisque — Bernkastler Doktor Riesling Auslese, 1982

With the Chicken — Freemark Abbey, Chardonnay, 1982

With the Dessert — Vintage Port Cockburn's, 1963

John B. Nowakowski, Executive Chef

Founded in December, 1983, Veronique's is the new kid on the block. Its home is the Biscayne Bay Marriott Hotel and Marina, overlooking, naturally, Biscayne Bay.

Enter this beautiful hotel, take the elevator to the second floor, and enter an elegant room filled with marble, Oriental artifacts, and etched glass depicting the restaurant's namesake, Lady Veronique. The burgundy-colored dining room is decorated with gleaming chandeliers and magnificent silk flowers.

It's the small touches that separate the good restaurant from the truly exceptional one. The small touches begin the moment you take your seat. Ladies receive satin pillows for their feet. Everyone receives complimentary caviar hor d'oeuvres, croissants, mid-meal sorbet, and coffee for two from a $1500 Hellem service. Specialties from the predominantly French bill of fare include lobster bisque, bouillabaisse "Marseillaise," and crêpes Suzette flambé.

"I went to the school of hard knocks," say 28-year-old chef John Nowakowski. The Baltimore-born chef began as a sous chef at the Marriott at Dallas Airport. Today he is in charge of all five kitchens at the chic Biscayne Bay Marriott Hotel.

1633 North Bayshore Drive

RADICCHIO AND BIBB LETTUCE SALAD
WITH TARRAGON DRESSING

1 head radicchio
2 heads bibb lettuce
   TARRAGON DRESSING
1 carrot, peeled and
   julienned

½ pound fresh
mushrooms washed and
thinly sliced
2 tomatoes, cut into wedges

1. Break the lettuces into leaves, wash, and spin dry.

2. Line four chilled salad plates with the radicchio leaves.

3. Mix the bibb lettuce with ¾ cup *TARRAGON DRESSING*, and arrange the salad on top of the radicchio.

4. Garnish each salad with the carrots, mushroom slices, and tomatoes.

Julienned means sliced into thin matchsticks. You can cut by hand or use the special shredding disk that comes with most food processors. Radicchio is a red-leafed lettuce that is very much in vogue. It looks like a head of red cabbage and costs ten times the price. It is available at specialty shops.

TARRAGON DRESSING

1 egg
2 tablespoons fresh tarragon
   leaves
½ ounce parsley sprigs
1½ teaspoons dry mustard
1½ teaspoons salt
1 tablespoon fresh lemon
   juice

1 clove garlic, finely
   chopped
1 shallot, finely chopped
⅔ cup tarragon vinegar
2½ cups salad oil

Combine all the ingredients except the oil in blender or food processor, and purée thoroughly at medium speed. When the mixture is smooth, add the oil in a *thin* stream. The sauce should thicken. This recipe makes 3 cups sauce.

This salad dressing is an emulsified sauce. Adding oil too quickly or blending too fast will cause the sauce to separate. To rescue a curdled sauce, try blending in a tablespoon of ice water. You must use fresh tarragon for this recipe. Fresh tarragon can be preserved in vinegar, however.

LOBSTER BISQUE

1 (10 ounce) lobster tail	3½ cups FISH STOCK (see page 167)
1 tablespoon peanut oil	Pinch of thyme
1 tablespoon clarified butter	1 bay leaf
1 celery stalk, finely diced	4 tablespoons butter
1 carrot, finely diced	4 tablespoons flour
1 ounce cognac	Salt and pepper to taste
2 tablespoons Spanish paprika	Splash Tabasco sauce
2 tablespoons tomato purée	¼ cup heavy cream
¼ cup dry white wine	

1. Cut the lobster tail, shell and all, into 1-inch pieces. Heat the oil and butter in a 2-quart saucepan over a moderate flame. Add the lobster and sauté until the shell becomes red. Add the vegetables and sauté until lightly browned. Add the cognac and ignite. Stir in the paprika, tomato purée, wine, stock, thyme, and bay leaf. Simmer for one hour.

2. Strain the bisque, reserving the lobster meat. Discard the shells and vegetables. Return the bisque to the heat. Make a roux: melt the butter in a small saucepan, the whisk in the flour. Cook the roux over medium heat for 2-3 minutes, but do not let brown. Working

off the heat, whisk the roux into the bisque, then gradually bring the bisque back to a boil, whisking constantly. Season with salt, pepper, and Tabasco sauce. Just before serving, whisk in the cream and reserve lobster meat.

This bisque is made with Florida lobster, which is also known as spiny lobster or langouste.

Roux should be cooked for at least two minutes to remove the floury taste. To avoid lumps, always add roux to a liquid off the heat.

CHICKEN ARMAGNAC

4 (6 ounce) boneless, skinless chicken breasts	2 tablespoons very finely chopped shallots
Salt and fresh black pepper	2 tablespoons Armagnac
1 cup flour	⅔ cup heavy cream
6 tablespoons clarified butter	2 tablespoons butter
4 jumbo shrimp, shelled and deveined	4 tablespoons finely chopped parsley

1. Pound the chicken breasts lightly between two sheets of moistened waxed paper. Season each with salt and pepper and dredge in flour, shaking off the excess. Heat 4 tablespoons clarified butter in a frying pan and sauté the chicken for two minutes per side, or until golden brown. Transfer to a platter and keep warm. Discard fat.

2. Melt the remaining clarified butter in the pan and sauté the shrimp for 1 minute, or until firm and pink. Remove the shrimp and keep warm. Add the shallots and cook over a low heat for 1 minute without browning. Add the Armagnac, increase the heat to high, and flambé. When the flame burns down, add the cream, and boil to reduce by half. Whisk in the butter and heat the sauce until bubbly.

3. Just before serving, warm the shrimp in the sauce and arrange one on each chicken breast, tail raised. Season the sauce with salt and pepper and pour it over the chicken. Garnish with parsley.

To flambé a sauce, heat the alcohol to body temperature and touch it with a live flame. If you are using gas heat, you need only tip the pan toward the flame. If you are using electric heat, hold a lit match 1 inch from the pan.

Armagnac is a grape brandy made in the southwest of France. Unlike cognac, it is only distilled once, producing a spirit with a more vigorous flavor.

PEARS BURGUNDY

4 ripe pears	3 tablespoons cold water
1 bottle Burgundian wine	A few drops fresh lemon
2 strips lemon zest (the	juice
outer peel)	VANILLA SAUCE
1 stick cinnamon	(see recipe below)
1 cup sugar	Fresh mint leaves for
1 tablespoon cornstarch	garnish

1. Peel the pears, leaving stems intact, and core them from the bottom. Place the pears in a saucepan with the wine, lemon zest, cinnamon, and sugar and gradually bring to a boil. Reduce the heat and gently simmer the pears for 5-8 minutes or until easily pierced with a skewer. Transfer pears to a platter and let cool.

2. Return the poaching liquid to the heat and boil until only 2 cups liquid remains. Mix the cornstarch and water to a smooth paste and whisk this mixture into the boiling wine. Remove from the heat and chill. Just before serving, whisk in lemon juice to taste.

3. Prepare the *VANILLA SAUCE*.

4. To assemble the dish, spoon the Burgundy sauce on the top half of each of four chilled dinner plates. Spoon the vanilla sauce on the bottom halves of the plates. Set the pears in the center. Garnish the stem end of each pear with a mint leaf.

This unusual pear dish comes with two sauces: one made from the red wine in which the pear is poached, the other from vanilla. We usually fill the pears with chocolate mousse, but to simplify the recipe, we have omitted it here.

VANILLA SAUCE

1 *cup plus 3 tablespoons milk*
¼ *cup granulated sugar*
1 *ounce vanilla powder*

2 *tablespoons brandy*
1 *cup heavy cream, lightly whipped*

1. Heat the milk and sugar in a small saucepan. Place three tablespoons milk in a small bowl and sprinkle the vanilla powder on top. Let stand for five minutes

2. Whisk the vanilla powder mixture into the remaining hot milk. Simmer, whisking gently, for three minutes, or until the mixture thickens. Remove from the heat and let cool. Just before serving, fold in the brandy and cream.

Note that this recipe is made with vanilla powder, not vanilla extract. Vanilla powder is available at select gourmet shops. One good brand is Snow White and Rose Red.

Vinton's

Dinner For Six

Tomato Surprise

Escalopes de Saumon a L'Oseille

Canard à la Framboise

Prommes au Gratin

Mousse au Chocolat

Wines:

With the Salmon — Louis Roederer Bruit Campagne

With the Duck — Châteauneuf–du–Pape

With the Mousse — Muscat de Beaumes–de–Venise

Hans Eichmann, Owner

Rene Madison, Owner, Chef

R ich in history, the La Palma Hotel once served as a rest and recreation center for officers of World War I. Today, it is the home of an internationally renown restaurant, Vinton's. Hans Eichman bought Vinton's from the original owner in 1971, waiting patiently for his brother, Rene, to join him in the kitchen. Rene finally came in 1977, a time Hans refers to as the "year of the great relief." Rene also proved to be the "comic relief," bringing an irrepressible sense of humor to the kitchen.

Hans and Rene are from a small town in Switzerland, near Zurich, where the Eichman family owned an inn. There were three brothers and one sister, and from an early age, working at the inn was a part of their lives. The brothers describe the Vinton's dining experience as "uptown food in a country setting." When asked about the restaurant's specialty, Rene replied "Whatever's flopping on the deck," mindful of Vinton's impeccable seafood.

Vinton's has everything: indoor dining in plum-colored rooms, private dining rooms tucked away for the romantically inclined, an outdoor courtyard where guests dine under colorful Martini and Rossi umbrellas. The "Old Florida" decor boasts antique paddle fans and Victorian linen lamps that pull up and down from the high ceilings. Monday night is gourmet night, featuring a fixed price, eight course feast. But any night, you can be assured of finding at Vinton's the finest in classical and contemporary French cuisine.

116 Alhambra Circle
Coral Gables

TOMATO SURPRISE

6 *ripe tomatoes*
3 *heads of Belgian endive*
2 *bunches of watercress*

SHERRY VINEGAR
DRESSING

1. Slice the top off the tomatoes and scoop out the insides.

2. Separate endive leaves and immerse them in warm water for a few seconds to remove bitterness and then in cold water to refresh them.

3. Place the tomatoes on individual plates and surround them with watercress. Stand the endive leaves in the hollow centers, larger ends down. Serve the *SHERRY VINEGAR DRESSING* on the side for dipping.

SHERRY VINEGAR DRESSING

1 *whole egg*
1 *tablespoon sherry vinegar*
1 *cup oil*

1 *tablespoon heavy cream*
Salt and pepper

Combine the egg and vinegar in a large bowl, and gradually whisk in the oil, followed by the cream and seasonings. Serve dressing in ramekins and dip the endive leaves into it.

This dressing tastes best when prepared at the last minute.

ESCALOPES DE SAUMON A L'OSEILLE
(Poached Salmon with Sorrel Sauce)

6 (6 ounce) salmon filets
2 quarts COURT-BOUILLON
1 cups FISH CREAM SAUCE

1 tomato, peeled, seeded, and chopped (see instructions on page 4)

1. Using a tweezer, remove all bones from the salmon. Heat the *COURT BOUILLON* in a fish poacher or large shallow pan just to a simmer—it should not boil. Place the salmon in the *COURT BOUILLON* and poach it for 3 minutes. Remove the pan from the heat and let sit for 2 minutes.

2. Transfer the salmon to a dish cloth to drain. Place each filet on a large plate and spoon the *FISH CREAM SAUCE* over it. Garnish each plate with diced tomato and a sorrel leaf.

Sorrel is an herb with a sour, lemony taste. It looks a little like spinach. There is no substitute for the flavor, but a fresh basil leaf would make an equally attractive garnish.

COURT-BOUILLON

6 cups water
2 cups white wine
1 carrot, peeled and sliced
1 onion, sliced
1 celery stalk, roughly chopped

6 peppercorns, crushed
1 bay leaf
1 tablespoon white vinegar

Combine all ingredients in a saucepan and bring to a boil. Lower heat and allow to simmer for 15 minutes. Strain

Court-Bouillon *means "short" or "quick bouillon," literally. Unlike stock, it can be made in 15 minutes.*

FISH CREAM SAUCE

4 *cups heavy cream*
2 *cups white wine*
2 *cups FISH STOCK (see*
   recipe on page 167)

1 *bunch sorrel*
Salt, white pepper,
   cayenne pepper

1. In a saucepan, bring the cream to a boil and reduce it to 2 cups. In another saucepan, reduce the wine to 1 cup. In a third saucepan, reduce the fish stock to 1 cup.

2. Combine all three ingredients in a food processor or blender and process until well mixed. Add the sorrel and process for 15-20 seconds. Strain the sauce and season it with salt, pepper, and cayenne. It should be thick and creamy.

CANARD A LA FRAMBOISE
(Roast Duck with Raspberry Sauce)

3 *ducks, about 5 pounds*
   each
3 *oranges*
1 *tablespoon dry oregano*

Salt and pepper
1 *bunch celery*
RASPBERRY SAUCE

1. Preheat the oven to 425°. Empty the duck's cavities. Cut the oranges in half and squeeze the juice over the birds. Put the squeezed oranges into the cavities for additional flavor. Sprinkle the ducks liberally with oregano, salt, and pepper.

2. Cover the bottom of a large roasting pan with the celery stalks. Place the ducks on the celery bed. Roast the ducks in the oven for 30 minutes. Lower the heat to 350° and continue roasting for 2½ hours. The ducks will be free of fat and very crisp. Cut the ducks in half lengthwise for serving, with the *RASPBERRY SAUCE* on the side.

RASPBERRY SAUCE

1 quart fresh raspberries or
   1 (10 ounce) package of
   thawed, frozen
   raspberries

¼ cup brandy
   Salt and pepper

Place the berries in a blender or food processor. Add the brandy, salt,and pepper, and purée. Strain the sauce to remove raspberry seeds. Warm the sauce gently, without boiling, before serving.

The celery serves three purposes: it adds flavor, prevents the ducks from sticking to the pan, and keeps them out of the fat.

POMMES AU GRATIN
(Gratin Potatoes)

6 large potatoes, peeled
1 medium onion
   Salt and pepper to taste

   A touch of grated nutmeg
   optional
6 tablespoons soft butter
1 quart heavy cream

1. Preheat the oven to 375°.

2. Cut the potatoes and the onion into thin slices. Combine the potatoes, onions, seasonings, butter and cream in a large mixing bowl and let stand for 10 minutes.

3. Butter a heavy roasting pan or oven-proof glass baking dish and spread ingredients neatly in it. Cover with foil and bake for one hour or until lightly brown. Cut the gratin into squares for serving.

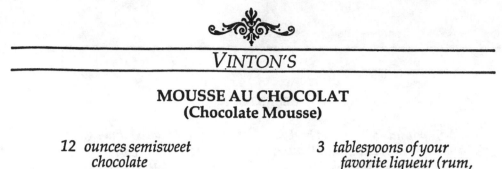

MOUSSE AU CHOCOLAT
(Chocolate Mousse)

12 ounces semisweet
     chocolate
12 eggs, separated
¾   cup cream
     Scant ½ cup sugar

3 tablespoons of your
   favorite liqueur (rum,
   cognac, kirsch, Grand
   Marnier, etc.)
6 strawberries
6 fresh mint leaves

1. Melt the chocolate in a double boiler over very low heat. Cool to room temperature.

2. Place the egg yolks, whites, and cream in three separate bowls. Beat the yolks with 3 tablespoons sugar until they are thick and form a ribbon when the whisk is lifted. Whip the cream with 2 tablespoons sugar. Beat the egg whites to stiff peaks, sprinkle in the remaining sugar as they thicken.

3. Fold the yolks into the melted, cooled chocolate with the liqueur. Gently fold in the egg whites and 1 cup of the whipped cream. Spoon the mousse into glasses and refrigerate for at least 24 hours.

4. Just before serving, decorate the mousse with rosettes of whipped cream, strawberries, and fresh mint leaves.

BEEF STOCK

4-5 pounds of veal and beef bones, cut in small pieces	1 large bouquet garni
2 onions, quartered	10 peppercorns
2 carrots, quartered	5 garlic cloves, unpeeled
2 stalks celery, cut in 2-inch pieces	1 tablespoon tomato paste
	3-4 quarts water

1. Put the bones into a roasting pan and roast in a very hot oven (450°) for 30-40 minutes, or until the bones are browned, stirring occasionally. Add the vegetables and brown them.

2. Transfer the bones and vegetables to a stock pot with a slotted spoon. Add the bouquet garni, peppercorns, garlic, tomato paste, water, and bring slowly to a boil. Skim any residue that forms on the top and simmer the stock for 4-5 hours. The stock should reduce very slowly.

3., Strain the stock. It can be kept in the refrigerator for 2 days or frozen.

CHICKEN STOCK

10 pounds chicken bones	4 carrots, peeled
2 large onions	1 bouquet garni
3 cloves	5 garlic cloves, unpeeled
2 stalks celery	½ bunch parsley
2 leeks, washed	

1. Cover the chicken bones with water in a large stock pot. Bring slowly to a boil and skim off any residue that forms on the surface. Cook for two hours.

2. Add the onions, cloves, celery, leeks, carrots, bouquet garni, garlic, parsley and cook at a slow boil for two more hours, adding water to the stock as it evaporates.

3. Strain the stock and reduce it to 3 quarts. Cool and refrigerate overnight. Remove any residue that forms on top of the stock.

FISH STOCK

1 tablespoon butter	1 quart water
1 medium-size onion, sliced	10 peppercorns
1½ pounds fish bones, cut into pieces	1 bouquet garni
	1 cup white wine

Melt the butter in a large stock pot, add the onions, and sauté until soft but not brown. Add the fish bones, water, peppercorns, bouquet garni, wine, and bring slowly to a boil, skimming any residue that forms on the surface. Simmer uncovered for 20 minutes, strain and season to taste.

Note: Do not bring stock to a rapid boil or it will become bitter. And never add skin as this darkens the stock.

ABOUT THE AUTHOR

Barbara Seldin Klein knows a thing or two about Miami restaurants. She is one of a rare breed of native Floridians, who was born and raised on Miami Beach. Her father owned Raphil's, a legendary Miami Beach deli whose regular customers included Milton Berle, Marlon Brando, and the infamous Meyer Lansky. When most children were still eating hotdogs, Ms. Seldin dined on sturgeon, caviar, and hand-sliced lox.

Ms. Seldin grew up during the golden age of Miami Beach, when the bumper to bumper traffic on Collins Avenue moved at a snail's pace and the rich and famous dined at such renowned restaurants as the Embers, Chandler's, and the Rascal House. She dined here not as a tourist, but as a native, which makes her uniquely qualified to write a book on Miami's best restaurants.

The Culinary Center of Vermont provided Ms. Seldin with an introduction to French cuisine. The year was 1979; the place was Stowe, Vermont; the instructors were some of the top cooking teachers from France. From there, it was on to Paris, where she attended the prestigious La Varenne cooking school. The following year her gastronomic investigations took her to Champagne, Burgundy, Bordeaux, and the southwest of France. On her return to the U.S., she founded her own business, the French Country Basket—a gourmet gift basket service ranked by South Florida Magazine as one of Miami's best.

Dining In Miami is Ms. Seldin's first book. To write it, she visited all 21 restaurants (plus several that did not pass the muster), dining with the owner, interviewing the chef, sometimes physically wresting the recipes from the kitchen. Today, she lives in South Miami with her two children, Jake and Betsy, dividing her time between Miami and Boston.

Appetizers

Artichokes Dolomiti (*Raimondo's*) 121
Asparagi All'Agro (*Tiberio*) 145
Clams Casino (*Palm*) 99
Coconut Shrimp (*Christine Lee's*) 19
Escargots with Rosemary (*Grand Cafe*) . 62
Mushrooms stuffed with Crabmeat
   (*New York Steak House*) 105
Oysters (*Chauveron*) 3
Ratatouille de Saumon aux
   Poivrons Rouges (*Spoonbill*) 139
Scallop Timables in Basil Sauce (*Forge*) . 50
Scampi (*Dining Galleries*) 27
Scrambled Eggs with Caviar (*Regine's*) . 130
Shrimp with Ginger Sauce
   (*Dominique's*) 34
Tomato Surprise (*Vinton's*) 161
Tortilla Española (*Casa Juancho*) 12

Beverages

Sangria (*Casa Juancho*) 11
Flaming Spanish Coffee
   (*New York Steak House*) 109

Dessert

Amaretto Soufflé (*Dominique's*) 36
Apple Pie (*Joe's*) 81
Blacksmith Pie (*Forge*) 56
Cheesecake (*Raimondo's*) 125
Chocolate-Dipped Strawberries
   (*Dining Galleries*) 29
Chocolate Mousse (*Vinton's*) 165
Chocolate Soufflé (*Chauveron*) 7
Chocolate Terrine (*Pavillon Grill*) 117
Dates stuffed with Turron and
   Marinated in Brandy (*El Sevilla*) . . . 45
Delices de Fraise et Framboise
   (*Grand Cafe*) 64

Key Lime Pie (*New York Steak House*) . 108
Leche Frita (*Casa Juancho*) 14
Marquise de Chocolat (*Regine's*) 133
Orange alla Cleopatra (*La Scala*) 88
Pears Burgundy (*Veronique's*) 156
Profitteroles (*Tiberio*) 148
Souffle Grand Marnier with
   Sabayon Sauce (*Le Festival*) 94
Strawberry Parfait (*Spoonbill*) 141
Zabaglione (*Il Tulipano*) 75

Entrees

Beef Tenderloin (*Grand Cafe*) 63
Chicken Armagnac(*Veronique's*) 155
Duckling Jubilee (*Forge*) 52
Frog Legs Provencale (*Chauvron*) 4
Lamb Medallions with
   Candied Garlic (*Regine's*) 131
Le Filet de Red Snapper Duglere
   (*Le Festival*) 93
Lemon Chicken (*Christine Lee's*) 21
Lobster (*Palm*) 101
Medallions of Veal with lemon Butter
   (*Pavillon*) 115
Medallions of Veal with Wild
   Mushroom Sauce (*Dominique's*) . . . 35
Merluza alla Vasca (*El Sevilla*) 42
Native Pompano (*Dining Galleries*) . . . 28
Paella (*Casa Juancho*) 13
Poached Salmon with Sorrel Sauce
   (*Vinton's*) 163
Roast Prime Ribs of Beef
   (*New York Steak House*) 107
Segoviana Style Suckling Pig
   (*El Sevilla*) 44
Shrimp Pancettati in Salsa Verde
   with Risotto(*Il Tulipano*) 72
Snapper with Shrimp and Vegetable
   (*La Scala*) 86
Spring Lobster Ragout (*Pavillon Grill*) . 114

RECIPE INDEX

Stone Crabs *(Joe's)* 79
Szechuan-Style Sliced Fish
   (Christine Lee's) 22
Tian de Filet d'Agneau aux Gouss d'Ail
   (Spoonbill) 140
Veal Chops Tre Corone *(Raimondo's)* . 124
Veal Francais *(La Scala)* 87
Veal Stuffed with Prosciutto and
   Mozzarella *(Il Tulipano)* 74

Pastas

Agnolotti Bandiera with Three Sauces
   (Il Tulipano) 69
Cannelloni Excelsior *(Raimondo's)* . . . 122
Linguine All'Aragosta *(Tiberio)* 147
White and Green Linguini with
   Vegetables and Ham *(La Scala)* 85

Salads

Fresh Garden Salad Bowl
   (New York Steak House) 106
Green Bean Salad with Truffle
   Vinaigrette *(Dominique's)* 33
La Salade Monte Carlo *(Le Festival)* . . . 93
Radicchio and Bibb Lettuce Salad with
   Tarragon Dressing *(Veronique's)* . . . 153
Salade de Rene *(Pavillon Grill)* 113
Salade Tropical *(Regine's)* 129
Seafood Salad "Costa del Sol"
   (El Sevilla) 41
Shrimp Merlin *(Forge)* 49

Salad Dressings

Easy Mayonnaise *(Forge)* 50
Italian Dressing
   (New York Steak House) 106
Mustard Sauce *(Joe's)* 79
Sherry Vinegar Dressing *(Vinton's)* . . 161

Tarragon Dressing *(Veronique's)* 153
Tropical Dressing *(Regine's)* 130
Truffle Vinaigrette *(Dominique's)* 34

Sauces and Stocks

Amaretto Sauce *(Dominique's)* 37
Basil Sauce *(Forge)* 51
Beef Stock 166
Bechamel Sauce *(El Sevilla)* 43
Brown Sauce *(Chauveron)* 5
Cherry Sauce *(Forge)* 53
Chicken Stock 166
Chocolate Sauce *(Tiberio)* 149
Coffee Sauce *(Regine's)* 135
Court Bouillon *(Vinton's)* 162
Cream Sauce *(Raimondo's)* 123
Demi Glace *(Forge)* 55
Fish Cream Sauce *(Vinton's)* 163
Fish Sauce *(Regine's)* 131
Fish Stock 167
Fresh Tomato Sauce *(Il Tulipano)* 70
Pesto Sauce *(Il Tulipano)* 71
Port Sauce *(Spoonbill)* 140
Raspberry Sauce *(Vinton's)* 164
Sabayon Sauce *(Le Festival)* 95
Salsa Verde *(Il Tulipano)* 73
Traditional Cream Sauce *(Il Tulipano)* . 70
Vanilla Sauce *(Veronique's)* 157

Soups

She Crab Soup *(Grand Cafe)* 61
Lobster Bisque *(Veronique's)* 154
Sopa de Ajo Castellana *(Casa Juancho)* . 11

Vegetables and Side Dishes

Candied Garlic *(Regine's)* 132
Cottage Fried Sweet Potatoes *(Joe's)* . . 80

RECIPE INDEX

Creamed Spinach
   (New York Steak House)   108
Eggplant Imperial *(Christine Lee's)* . . .   20
Glazed Carrots *(Dining Galleries)*   29
Gratin Potatoes *(Vinton's)*   164
Grilled Tomatoes *(Joe's)*   80
Mozzarella Bella *(Tiberio)*   146
Onion Rings *(Palm)*   100
Pommes Soufflées *(Chauveron)*   6
Risotto *(Il Tulipano)*   73
Spatzle *(Forge)*   56

DINING IN-WITH THE GREAT CHEFS

A Collection of Gourmet Recipes from the Finest Chefs in the Country

Each book contains gourmet recipes for complete meals from the chefs of 21 great restaurants.

___ *Dining In–Baltimore* $7.95	___ *Dining In–Monterey Peninsula* 7.95
___ *Dining In–Boston (Revised)* 8.95	___ *Dining In–New Orleans* 8.95
___ *Dining In–Chicago, Vol. III* 8.95	___ *Dining In–Philadelphia* 8.95
___ *Dining In–Cleveland* 8.95	___ *Dining In–Phoenix* 8.95
___ *Dining In–Dallas (Revised)* 8.95	___ *Dining In–Pittsburgh (Revised)* 7.95
___ *Dining In–Denver* 7.95	___ *Dining In–Portland* 7.95
___ *Dining In–Hampton Roads* 8.95	___ *Dining In–St. Louis* 7.95
___ *Dining In–Hawaii* 7.95	___ *Dining In–Salt Lake City* 8.95
___ *Dining In–Houston, Vol. II* 7.95	___ *Dining In–San Francisco, Vol II* 7.95
___ *Dining In–Kansas City (Revised)* 7.95	___ *Dining In–Seattle* 8.95
___ *Dining In–Los Angeles (Revised)* 8.95	___ *Dining In–Sun Valley* 7.95
___ *Dining In–Manhattan* 8.95	___ *Dining In–Toronto* 7.95
___ *Dining In–Miami* 8.95	___ *Dining In–Vancouver, B.C.* 8.95
___ *Dining In–Milwaukee* 7.95	___ *Dining In–Washington, D.C.* 8.95
___ *Dining In–Minneapolis/St. Paul, Vol. II* . . $8.95	

☐ Check here if you would like to have a different Dining In–Cookbook sent to you once a month. Payable by MasterCard or VISA. Returnable if not satisfied.

☐ Payment enclosed $_____ (Please include $1.00 postage and handling for each book)

☐ Charge to:

Visa # _____ Exp. Date _____

MasterCard # _____ Exp. Date _____

Signature _____

Name _____

Address _____

City _____ State _____ Zip _____

SHIP TO (if other than name and address above):

Name _____

Address _____

City _____ State _____ Zip _____

PEANUT BUTTER PUBLISHING

911 Western Avenue, Suite 401, Maritime Building ▪ Seattle, WA 98104 ▪ (206) 628-6200